THE GOSPEL

SCHOCKEN BOOKS · NEW YORK

BAIRD W. WHITLOCK

The GOSPEL

The Life of Jesus

First published by Schocken Books 1984

10 9 8 7 6 5 4 3 2 1   84 85 86 87

Library of Congress Cataloging in Publication Data
Whitlock, Baird W.
The Gospel.
1. Jesus Christ—Biography—Sources, Biblical.
I. Bible. N.T. Gospels. English. Authorized.
II. Title.
BT299.2.W46   1984   226'.1   83–40471

Designed by Lynn Braswell

Manufactured in the United States of America

ISBN 0–8052–3875–1

Preface

When I was growing up, I often heard older people say that there were discrepancies in the stories of the Bible that could not be reconciled. Usually I found that what they were doing was taking individual quotes like "Eat, drink, and be merry" and using them out of context. Sometimes, of course, they were talking about the real ambiguities in biblical translation about such things as taking other people's lives. But I suppose that one of the most repeated examples which my elders used involved the resurrection accounts. I had an uncle who simply took for granted that there was no way to reconcile the four Gospels. Later, during college, I read Samuel Butler's *The Way of All Flesh* and ran into Ernest Pontifex's long personal attempt to reconcile the accounts: "When he had finished Dean Alford's notes he found them come to this, namely, that no one yet had succeeded in bringing the four accounts into tolerable harmony with each other, and that the Dean, seeing no chance of succeeding better than his predecessors had done, recommended that the whole story should be taken on trust—and this Ernest was not prepared to do."

I thought then that I should try my own hand at the task, but as with so many good intentions, I didn't get around to it but kept putting it off as a worthwhile future Lenten exercise. Last year, I finally got to it and found not only that it was possible, but that such a reconciliation of the texts brought about a possible deeper understanding of the relationship of Jesus and Mary Magdalene and cleared up some of the seeming inconsistencies in individual accounts.

This exercise then carried me into a consideration of something else I had often heard, which was that although Matthew, Mark, and Luke, the "synoptic" Gospels, showed some actual relationships, John stood apart from them and simply wouldn't fit with them. That situation offered a further challenge: was it possible to reconcile the four Gospels into one continuous narrative?

Such a challenge also related to another feeling that I had about much biblical criticism, especially that stemming from the nineteenth century. It seemed to me to involve a false use of Kantian logic based on the concept that if you wish to find out what is genuinely historical or "real" in the gospel accounts, you look for what is present or repeated in all four (or three, or even two) Gospels, rather than accepting all the unique occurrences as well. That seemed to me to be a false kind of reductionist thinking. If four of my friends were to go to a speech that I was unable to attend, I would not, if I wanted to find out what was said, take for granted that the only things the speaker had said were those that all four of my friends remembered in common. I would much more likely find out the true content of the speech by putting together their full accounts, not only what they all said in common but what they all remembered *in toto*. If they disagreed on anything, that would, of course, present a real problem. But if they backed up each other's memories and gave a fuller idea of the speaker's points, then I would be getting closer to the actual speech.

Such an amplification seemed to me to be one possible value of trying to find out if a full reconciliation of the Gospels was possible. And it was with such a goal in mind that I set to work. I had always been struck by the fact that those who emphasized the differences between the Gospels always used those differences as a way of "explaining away" passages they did not like and did not agree with for various reasons. That struck me as a dubious approach for those who were otherwise perfectly content with using phrases like "The Word of God" in describing the Bible.

I was also perfectly aware of the warning contained in the "Revelation": "If any man shall add unto these things, God shall add unto him the plagues that are written in this book: and if any man shall take away from the words of the book of this prophecy, God shall take away his part out of the book of life, and out of the holy city, and *from* the things which are written in this book." That seemed to me a warning that was worth heeding when dealing with a reworking of the text.

Next there was the problem of choosing which words to use in bringing the accounts together. One choice would be to do a new translation after uniting the Greek passages. Although this was a tantalizing choice, I rejected it, at least on the first go around, because my purpose was to present a combined gospel that people would not only find helpful but would want to read. For that reason I decided to stick with the King James Version. It remains the most beautiful and most readable text, as well as the most familiar. It is also a superb translation, whose only major drawback is that the meaning of many seventeenth-century words has changed. It is my belief that most readers are well aware of that drawback, and if they are interested enough to read the Gospels at length, they are interested enough to look up words that would cause trouble. If enough readers find the continuous narrative worth reading, then a more modern rendering could follow.

There was, of course, the all-important question: why do it at all? There seems to me a very practical answer to that. Most readers are perfectly aware that the gospels give varying pictures of the words and life of Jesus. With enough work, and with the help of many books that outline the comparative passages of the various Gospels, a reader can do his or her own reconciliation of various passages. But I soon found that bringing the accounts together had an added benefit. The wording became much richer when pulled together. The logic of the sequence of various passages, like the Sermon on the Mount, became clearer when the various parallel passages were brought together. Even the reason for various events, such as the breaking up of the crowd following the feeding of the five thousand, took on new significance when the passages were joined.

One short passage will show how the richness of texture is increased when two different accounts are joined together. The example I have chosen here is the parable of the House founded upon the Rock:

Matthew	*The Gospel*	*Luke*
Therefore whosoever heareth these sayings of mine, and doeth them, I will liken him unto a wise man, which built his house upon a rock: and the rain descended, and the floods came, and the winds blew, and beat upon that house; and it fell not: for it was founded upon a rock. And every one that heareth these sayings of mine, and doeth them not, shall be likened unto a foolish man, which built his house upon the sand: and the rain descended, and the floods came, and the winds blew, and beat upon that house; and it fell: and great was the fall of it.	Therefore whosoever cometh to me, and heareth my sayings, and doeth them, I will shew you to whom he is like: he is like a wise man which built an house, and digged deep, and laid the foundation on a rock: and the rain descended, and the floods arose, and the winds blew, and the stream beat vehemently upon that house, and could not shake it, and it fell not: for it was founded upon a rock. But every one that heareth these sayings of mine, and doeth them not, shall be likened unto a foolish man that without a foundation built his house upon the sand:	Whosoever cometh to me, and heareth my sayings, and doeth them, I will shew you to whom he is like: he is like a man which built an house, and digged deep, and laid the foundation on a rock: and when the flood arose, the stream beat vehemently upon that house, and could not shake it: for it was founded upon a rock. But he that heareth and doeth not, is like a man that without a foundation built an house upon the earth; against which the stream did beat vehemently, and immediately it fell; and the ruin of that house was great.

Matthew	The Gospel	Luke
	and the rains descended, and the floods came, and the winds blew, and the stream did beat vehemently upon that house: and immediately it fell: and great was the fall of it.	

Two benefits are gained by bringing the Gospels together, then. The first is to bring together in one narrative all of the events of Jesus' life without having to search from one gospel to the other. The other is to gain the richness of the combined stories and statements. In the process I have tried to avoid all unnecessary repetition except when the contexts themselves indicate that Jesus said the same thing two or more times in different contexts; but I have also included all of the language of the various Gospels. If I have done my job well, nothing has been left out. I have even included variant wordings when it was not possible to combine the language exactly.

In deciding upon the order of the events in the narrative, I have not followed any particular scholar or group of scholars. I have tried as much as possible to let the logic of the events from the Gospels themselves lead me. At one time one gospel leads the way; at another, a different gospel. I have attempted not to let any personal prejudices or theological positions impose themselves. To my delight and often to my great surprise, unexpected elements have appeared to help me. The best example is the problem of where to place the mystery chapters of the Gospel of John, Chapters 7 through 10. It was not at all clear to me at the beginning where they should go. Then the fact that they took place in Jerusalem during the late autumn and early winter, during the feasts of Tabernacles in October and the Feast of the Dedication, now known as Hanukkah, a little over a month later, dictated the position I have given them, for all of the other events referred to in those chapters fit clearly either before or after that period in the first year of his ministry.

I claim no infallibility in the order here presented. I do not claim that all of the passages I have amalgamated were actually spoken at one time, nor that those apparently close in wording were spoken more than once as I have placed them. In each case the events seemed to me to call for the treatment I have given them. I can only prayerfully hope that I have come close to the real situation. There is, of necessity, an implied historical chronology, beginning before one Passover and running through the third Passover. That is longer than some critics claim for the length of Jesus' ministry and shorter than the traditional view of three years. To shorten the period would have required a decision that John was not accurate in his time statements; to lengthen the period would have required an editorial decision to insert a sequence I could not find in the texts themselves. To repeat, all of the wording of the four Gospels is included in this text.

My intention has never been to replace the accepted canon; it has been to present a single, continuous narrative that readers would find interesting, valuable, and enjoyable. I hope that this version will lead the reader back to the standard Gospels with some new insights. If it also moves anyone who has not read all of Matthew, Mark, Luke, and John to complete the entire gospel story, it will have achieved its goal.

THE GOSPEL

Forasmuch as many have taken in hand to set forth in order a declaration of those things which are most surely believed among us, even as they delivered them unto us, which from the beginning were eyewitnesses, and ministers of the word; it seemed good to me also, having had perfect understanding of all things from the very first, to write unto thee in order, most excellent Theophilus, that thou mightest know the certainty of those things, wherein thou hast been instructed.

THE WORD

In the beginning was the Word, and the Word was with God, and the Word was God. The same was in the beginning with God. All things were made by him; and without him was not any thing made that was made. In him was life; and the life was the light of men. And the light shineth in darkness; and the darkness comprehended it not.

There was a man sent from God, whose name *was* John. The same came for a witness, to bear witness of the Light, that all *men* through him might believe. He was not that Light, but *was sent* to bear witness of that Light. *That* was the true Light, which lighteth every man that cometh into the world. He was in the world, and the world was made by him, and the world knew him not. He came unto his own, and his own received him not. But as many as received him, to them gave he power to become the sons of God, *even* to them that believe on his name: which were born, not of blood, nor of the will of the flesh, nor of the will of man, but of God. And the Word was made flesh, and dwelt among us, (and we beheld his glory, the glory as of the only begotten of the Father,) full of grace and truth.

John bare witness of him, and cried, saying, "This was he of whom I spake, 'He that cometh after me is preferred before me: for he was before me.'" And of his fulness have all we received, and grace for grace. For the law was given by Moses, *but* grace and truth came by Jesus Christ. No man hath seen God at any time; the only begotten Son, which is in the bosom of the Father, he hath declared *him*.

THE CONCEPTION OF JOHN THE BAPTIST

There was in the days of Herod, the king of Judaea, a certain priest named Zacharias, of the course of Abia: and his wife *was* of the daughters of Aaron, and her name *was* Elisabeth. And they were both righteous before God, walking in all the commandments and ordinances of the Lord blameless. And they had no child, because that Elisabeth was barren, and they both were *now* well stricken in years. And it came to pass, that while he executed the priest's office before God in the order of his course, according to the custom of the priest's office, his lot was to burn incense when he went into the temple of the Lord. And the whole multitude of the people were praying without at the time of incense. And there appeared unto him an angel of the Lord standing on the right side of the altar of incense. And when Zacharias saw *him*, he was troubled, and fear fell upon him. But the angel said unto him, "Fear not, Zacharias: for thy prayer is heard; and thy wife Elisabeth shall bear thee a son, and thou shalt call his name John. And thou shalt have joy and gladness; and many shall rejoice at his birth. For he shall be great in the sight of the Lord, and shall drink neither wine nor strong drink; and he shall be filled with the Holy Ghost, even from his mother's womb. And many of the children of Israel shall he turn to the Lord their God. And he shall go before him in the spirit and power of Elias, to turn the hearts of the fathers to the children, and the disobedient to the wisdom of the just; to make ready a people prepared for the Lord." And Zacharias said unto the angel, "Whereby shall I know this? for I am an old man, and my wife well stricken in years." And the angel answering said unto him, "I am Gabriel, that stand in the presence of God; and am sent to speak unto thee, and to shew thee these glad tidings. And, behold, thou shalt be dumb, and not able to speak, until the day that these things shall be performed, because thou believest not my words, which shall be fulfilled in their season." And the people waited for Zacharias, and marvelled that he tarried so long in the temple. And when he came out, he could not speak unto them: and they perceived that he had seen a vision in the temple: for he beckoned unto them, and remained speechless. And it came to pass, that, as soon as the days of his ministration were accomplished, he departed to his own house. And after those days his wife Elisabeth conceived, and hid herself five months, saying, "Thus hath the Lord dealt with me in the days wherein he looked on *me*, to take away my reproach among men."

THE ANNUNCIATION AND VISITATION

And in the sixth month the angel Gabriel was sent from God unto a city of Galilee, named Nazareth, to a virgin espoused to a man whose name was Joseph, of the house of David; and the virgin's name *was* Mary. And the angel came in unto her, and said, "Hail, *thou that art* highly favoured, the Lord *is* with thee: blessed *art* thou among women." And when she saw *him*, she was troubled at his saying, and cast in her mind what manner of salutation this should be. And the angel said unto her, "Fear not, Mary: for thou hast found favour with God. And, behold, thou shalt conceive in thy womb, and bring forth a son, and shalt call his name JESUS. He shall be great, and shall be called the Son of the Highest: and the Lord God shall give unto him the throne of his father David: and he shall reign over the house of Jacob for ever; and of his kingdom there shall be no end." Then said Mary unto the angel, "How shall this be, seeing I know not a man?" And the angel answered and said unto her, "The Holy Ghost shall come upon thee, and the power of the Highest shall overshadow thee: therefore also that holy thing which shall be born of thee shall be called the Son of God. And, behold, thy cousin Elisabeth, she hath also conceived a son in her old age: and this is the sixth month with her, who was called barren. For with God nothing shall be impossible." And Mary said, "Behold the handmaid of the Lord; be it unto me according to thy word." And the angel departed from her.

MARY VISITS ELISABETH (*Magnificat*)

And Mary arose in those days, and went into the hill country with haste, into a city of Juda; and entered into the house of Zacharias, and saluted Elisabeth. And it came to pass, that, when Elisabeth heard the salutation of Mary, the babe leaped in her womb; and Elisabeth was filled with the Holy Ghost: and she spake out with a loud voice, and said, "Blessed *art* thou among women, and blessed *is* the fruit of thy womb. And whence *is* this to me, that the mother of my Lord should come to me? For, lo, as soon as the voice of thy salutation sounded in mine ears, the babe leaped in my womb for joy. And blessed *is* she that believed: for there shall be a performance of those things which were told her from the Lord."

And Mary said, "My soul doth magnify the Lord, and my spirit hath rejoiced in God my Saviour. For he hath regarded the low estate of his handmaiden: for, behold, from henceforth all generations shall call me blessed. For he that is mighty hath done to me great things; and holy *is* his name. And his mercy *is* on them that fear him from generation to generation. He hath shewed strength with his arm; he hath scattered the proud in the imagination of their hearts. He hath put down the mighty from *their* seats, and exalted them of low degree. He hath filled the hungry with good things; and the rich he hath sent empty away. He hath holpen his servant Israel, in remembrance of *his* mercy; as he spake to our fathers, to Abraham, and to his seed for ever." And Mary abode with her about three months, and returned to her own house.

THE ANGEL APPEARS TO JOSEPH

Now the birth of Jesus Christ was on this wise: When as his mother Mary was espoused to Joseph, before they came together, she was found with child of the Holy Ghost. Then Joseph her husband, being a just *man*, and not willing to make her a publick example, was minded to put her away privily. But while he thought on these things, behold, the angel of the Lord appeared unto him in a dream, saying, "Joseph, thou son of David, fear not to take unto thee Mary thy wife: for that which is conceived in her is of the Holy Ghost. And she shall bring forth a son, and thou shalt call his name JESUS: for he shall save his people from their sins."

Now all this was done, that it might be fulfilled which was spoken of the Lord by the prophet, saying, "Behold, a virgin shall be with child, and shall bring forth a son, and they shall call his name Emmanuel, which being interpreted is, 'God with us.' " Then Joseph being raised from sleep did as the angel of the Lord had bidden him, and took unto him his wife: and knew her not till she had brought forth her firstborn son: and he called his name JESUS.

THE BIRTH OF JOHN

Now Elisabeth's full time came that she should be delivered; and she brought forth a son. And her neighbours and her cousins heard how the Lord had shewed great mercy upon her; and they rejoiced with her. And it came to pass, that on the eighth day they came to circumcise the child; and they called him Zacharias, after the name of his father. And his mother answered and said, "Not *so*; but he shall be called John." And they said unto her, "There is none of thy kindred that is called by this name." And they made signs to his father, how he would have him called. And he asked for a writing table, and wrote, saying, "His name is John." And they marvelled all.

(Benedictus)

And his mouth was opened immediately, and his tongue *loosed*, and he spake, and praised God. And fear came on all that dwelt round about them: and all these sayings were noised abroad throughout all the hill country of Judaea. And all they that heard *them* laid *them* up in their hearts, saying, "What manner of child shall this be?" And the hand of the Lord was with him. And his father Zacharias was filled with the Holy Ghost, and prophesied, saying, "Blessed *be* the Lord God of Israel; for he hath visited and redeemed his people. And hath raised up an horn of salvation for us in the house of his servant David; as he spake by the mouth of his holy prophets, which have been since the world began: that we should be saved from our enemies, and from the hand of all that hate us; to perform the mercy *promised* to our fathers, and to remember his holy covenant; the oath which he sware to our father Abraham, that he would grant unto us, that we being delivered out of the hand of our enemies might serve him without fear, in holiness and righteousness before him, all the days of our life. And thou, child, shalt be called the prophet of the Highest: for thou shalt go before the face of the Lord to prepare his ways; to give knowledge of salvation unto his people by the remission of their sins, through the tender mercy of our God; whereby the dayspring from on high hath visited us, to give light to them that sit in darkness and *in* the shadow of death, to guide our feet into the way of peace." And the child grew, and waxed strong in spirit, and was in the deserts till the day of his shewing unto Israel.

THE BIRTH OF JESUS
(THE CHRISTMAS STORY)

And it came to pass in those days, that there went out a decree from Caesar Augustus, that all the world should be taxed. (*And* this taxing was first made when Cyrenius was governor of Syria.) And all went to be taxed, every one into his own city. And Joseph also went up from Galilee, out of the city of Nazareth, into Judaea, unto the city of David, which is called Bethlehem; (because he was of the house and lineage of David:) to be taxed with Mary his espoused wife, being great with child. And so it was, that, while they were there, the days were accomplished that she should be delivered. And she brought forth her firstborn son, and wrapped him in swaddling clothes, and laid him in a manger; because there was no room for them in the inn.

And there were in the same country shepherds abiding in the field, keeping watch over their flock by night. And, lo, the angel of the Lord came upon them, and the glory of the Lord shone round about them: and they were sore afraid. And the angel said unto them, "Fear not: for, behold, I bring you good tidings of great joy, which shall be to all people. For unto you is born this day in the city of David a Saviour, which is Christ the Lord. And this *shall be* a sign unto you: Ye shall find the babe wrapped in swaddling clothes, lying in a manger." And suddenly there was with the angel a multitude of the heavenly host praising God, and saying, "Glory to God in the highest, and on earth peace, good will toward men." And it came to pass, as the angels were gone away from them into heaven, the shepherds said one to another, "Let us now go even unto Bethlehem, and see this thing which is come to pass, which the Lord hath made known to us." And they came with haste, and found Mary, and Joseph, and the babe lying in a manger. And when they had seen *it*, they made known abroad the saying which was told them concerning this child. And all they that heard *it* wondered at those things which were told them by the shepherds. But Mary kept all these things, and pondered *them* in her heart. And the shepherds returned, glorifying and praising God for all the things that they had heard and seen, as it was told unto them. And when eight days were accomplished for the circumcising of the child, his name was called JESUS, which was so named of the angel before he was conceived in the womb.

THE COMING OF THE MAGI

Now when Jesus was born in Bethlehem of Judaea in the days of Herod the king, behold, there came wise men from the east to Jerusalem, saying, "Where is he that is born King of the Jews? for we have seen his star in the east, and are come to worship him." When Herod the king had heard *these things*, he was troubled, and all Jerusalem with him. And when he had gathered all the chief priests and scribes of the people together, he demanded of them where Christ should be born. And they said unto him, "In

Bethlehem of Judaea: for thus it is written by the prophet, 'And thou Bethlehem, *in* the land of Juda, art not the least among the princes of Juda: for out of thee shall come a Governor, that shall rule my people Israel.' " Then Herod, when he had privily called the wise men, enquired of them diligently what time the star appeared. And he sent them to Bethlehem, and said, "Go and search diligently for the young child; and when ye have found *him*, bring me word again, that I may come and worship him also." When they had heard the king, they departed; and, lo, the star, which they saw in the east, went before them, till it came and stood over where the young child was. When they saw the star, they rejoiced with exceeding great joy. And when they were come into the house, they saw the young child with Mary his mother, and fell down, and worshipped him: and when they had opened their treasures, they presented unto him gifts; gold, and frankincense, and myrrh. And being warned of God in a dream that they should not return to Herod, they departed into their own country another way.

THE PRESENTATION AT THE TEMPLE (*Nunc Dimittis*)

And when the days of her purification were accomplished according to the law of Moses, they brought him to Jerusalem, to present *him* to the Lord; (As it is written in the law of the Lord, "Every male that openeth the womb shall be called holy to the Lord";) and to offer a sacrifice according to that which is said in the law of the Lord, "A pair of turtledoves, or two young pigeons." And, behold, there was a man in Jerusalem, whose name *was* Simeon; and the same man *was* just and devout, waiting for the consolation of Israel: and the Holy Ghost was upon him. And it was revealed unto him by the Holy Ghost, that he should not see death, before he had seen the Lord's Christ. And he came by the Spirit into the temple: and when the parents brought in the child Jesus, to do for him after the custom of the law, then took he him up in his arms, and blessed God, and said, "Lord, now lettest thou thy servant depart in peace, according to thy word: for mine eyes have seen thy salvation, which thou hast prepared before the face of all people; a light to lighten the Gentiles, and the glory of thy people Israel." And Joseph and his mother marvelled at those things which were spoken of him. And Simeon blessed them, and said unto Mary his mother, "Behold, this *child* is set for the fall and rising again of many in Israel; and for a sign which shall be spoken against; (Yea, a sword shall pierce through thy own soul also,) that the thoughts of many hearts may be revealed."

And there was one Anna, a prophetess, the daughter of Phanuel, of the tribe of Aser: she was of a great age, and had lived with an husband seven years from her virginity; and she *was* a widow of about fourscore and four years, which departed not from the temple, but served *God* with fastings and prayers night and day. And she coming in that instant gave thanks likewise unto the Lord, and spake of him to all that looked for redemption in Jerusalem. And when they had performed all things according to the law of the Lord, they returned into Galilee, to their own city Nazareth.

THE SLAYING OF THE INNOCENTS AND FLIGHT TO EGYPT

And when they [the wise men] were departed, behold, the angel of the Lord appeareth to Joseph in a dream, saying, "Arise, and take the young child and his mother, and flee into Egypt, and be thou there until I bring thee word: for Herod will seek the young child to destroy him." When he arose, he took the young child and his mother by night, and departed into Egypt: and was there until the death of Herod: that it might be fulfilled which was spoken of the Lord by the prophet, saying, "Out of Egypt have I called my son."

Then Herod, when he saw that he was mocked of the wise

men, was exceeding wroth, and sent forth, and slew all the children that were in Bethlehem, and in all the coasts thereof, from two years old and under, according to the time which he had diligently enquired of the wise men. Then was fulfilled that which was spoken by Jeremy the prophet, saying, "In Rama was there a voice heard, lamentation, and weeping, and great mourning. Rachel weeping *for* her children, and would not be comforted, because they are not."

But when Herod was dead, behold, an angel of the Lord appeareth in a dream to Joseph in Egypt, saying, "Arise, and take the young child and his mother, and go into the land of Israel: for they are dead which sought the young child's life. And he arose, and took the young child and his mother, and came into the land of Israel. But when he heard that Archelaus did reign in Judaea in the room of his father Herod, he was afraid to go thither: notwithstanding, being warned of God in a dream, he turned aside into the parts of Galilee: and he came and dwelt in a city called Nazareth: that it might be fulfilled which was spoken by the prophets, "He shall be called a Nazarene."

IN THE TEMPLE

And the child grew, and waxed strong in spirit, filled with wisdom: and the grace of God was upon him. Now his parents went to Jerusalem every year at the feast of the passover. And when he was twelve years old, they went up to Jerusalem after the custom of the feast. And when they had fulfilled the days, as they returned, the child Jesus tarried behind in Jerusalem; and Joseph and his mother knew not *of it*. But they, supposing him to have been in the company, went a day's journey; and they sought him among *their* kinsfolk and acquaintance. And when they found him not, they turned back again to Jerusalem, seeking him. And it came to pass, that after three days they found him in the temple, sitting in the midst of the doctors, both hearing them, and asking them questions. And all that heard him were astonished at his understanding and answers. And when they saw him, they were amazed: and his mother said unto him, "Son, why hast thou thus dealt with us? behold, thy father and I have sought thee sorrowing." And he said unto them, "How is it that ye sought me? wist ye not that I must be about my Father's business?" And they understood not the saying which he spake unto them. And he went down with them, and came to Nazareth, and was subject unto them: but his mother kept all these sayings in her heart. And Jesus increased in wisdom and stature, and in favour with God and man.

THE PREACHING OF JOHN

Now in the fifteenth year of the reign of Tiberius Caesar, Pontius Pilate being governor of Judaea, and Herod being tetrarch of Galilee, and his brother Philip tetrarch of Ituraea and of the region of Trachonitis, and Lysanias the tetrarch of Abilene, Annas and Caiaphas being the high priests, the word of God came unto John the son of Zacharias in the wilderness of Judaea. And he came into all the country about Jordan, preaching the baptism of repentance for the remission of sins, saying, "Repent ye: for the kingdom of heaven is at hand"; for this is he that was spoken of by the prophet Esaias, "Behold, I send my messenger before thy face, which shall prepare thy way before thee. The voice of one crying in the wilderness, 'Prepare ye the way of the Lord, make his paths straight.' Every valley shall be filled, and every mountain and hill shall be brought low; and the crooked shall be made straight, and the rough ways *shall be* made smooth; and all flesh shall see the salvation of God." And John was clothed with camel's hair, and with a girdle of a skin about his loins; and he did eat locusts and wild honey. Then went out to him Jerusalem, and all Judaea, and all the region round about Jordan, and were baptized of him in Jordan, confessing their sins.

But when he saw many of the Pharisees and Sadducees come to his baptism, he said unto them, "O generation of vipers, who hath warned you to flee from the wrath to come? Bring forth therefore fruits meet for repentance: and think not to say within yourselves, 'We have Abraham to *our* father': for I say unto you, that God is able of these stones to raise up children unto Abraham. And now also the axe is laid unto the root of the trees: therefore every tree which bringeth forth not good fruit is hewn down, and cast into the fire." And the people asked him, saying, "What shall we do then?" He answereth and saith unto them, "He that hath two coats, let him impart to him that hath none; and he that hath meat, let him do likewise." Then came also publicans to be baptized, and said unto him, "Master, what shall we do?" And he said unto them, "Exact no more than that which is appointed you." And the soldiers likewise demanded of him, saying, "And what shall we do?" and he said unto them, "Do violence to no man, neither accuse *any* falsely; and be content with your wages." And many other things in his exhortation preached he unto the people. And the people were in expectation, and all men mused in their hearts of John, whether he were the Christ or not.

JOHN WITNESSES OF THE COMING CHRIST

And this is the record of John, when the Jews sent priests and Levites from Jerusalem to ask him, "Who art thou?" And he confessed, and denied not; but confessed, "I am not the Christ." And they asked him, "What then? Art thou Elias?" And he saith, "I am not." "Art thou that prophet?" And he answered, "No." Then said they unto him, "Who art thou? that we may give an answer to them that sent us. What sayest thou of thyself?" He said, "I *am* the voice of one crying in the wilderness. Make straight the way of the Lord, as said the prophet Esaias." And they which were sent were of the Pharisees. And they asked him, and said unto him, "Why baptizest thou then, if thou be not that Christ, nor Elias, neither that prophet?" John answered them, saying, "I baptize with water unto repentance: but there standeth one among you, whom ye know not; he shall baptize you with the Holy Ghost, and *with* fire. He it is, who coming after me is mightier than I [preferred before me—John], whose shoe's latchet I am not worthy to stoop down and unloose [whose shoes I am not worthy to bear—Matthew], whose fan *is* in his hand, and he will thoroughly purge his floor, and gather his wheat into the garner; but he will burn up the chaff with unquenchable fire."

THE BAPTISM OF JESUS

These things were done in Bethabara beyond Jordan, where John was baptizing. The next day, when all the people were baptized, Jesus cometh from Nazareth of Galilee to Jordan unto John. John seeth Jesus coming unto him, and saith, "Behold the Lamb of God, which taketh away the sin of the world. This is he of whom I said, 'After me cometh a man which is preferred before me: for he was before me.' And I knew him not: but that he should be made manifest to Israel, therefore am I come baptizing with water."

Then Jesus cometh to be baptized of him. But John forbad him, saying, "I have need to be baptized of thee, and comest thou to me?" And Jesus answering said unto him, "Suffer *it to be so* now: for thus it becometh us to fulfil all righteousness." Then he suffered him. And Jesus, when he was baptized and prayed, went up straightway out of the water: and, lo, the heavens were opened unto him, and he saw the Spirit of God descending in a bodily shape like a dove, and lighting upon him: and lo a voice from heaven saying, "Thou art [This is—Matthew] my beloved Son, in whom I am well pleased." And John bare record, saying, "I saw the Spirit descending from heaven like a dove, and it abode upon him. And I knew him not: but he that sent me to baptize with water, the same said unto me, 'Upon whom thou shalt see the Spirit descending, and remaining on him, the same is he which baptizeth with the Holy Ghost.' And I saw, and bare record that this is the Son of God."

THE TEMPTATION

And Jesus being full of the Holy Ghost returned from Jordan, and was led by the Spirit into the wilderness to be tempted of the devil, and was with the wild beasts. And when he had fasted forty days and forty nights, he was afterward an hungred.* And when the tempter came to him, he said, "If thou be the Son of God, command that these stones be made bread." But he answered and said, "It is written, 'Man shall not live by bread alone, but by every word that proceedeth out of the mouth of God.' " Then the devil taketh him up into the holy city, Jerusalem, and setteth him on a pinnacle of the temple, and saith unto him, "If thou be the Son of God, cast thyself down from hence: for it is written, 'He shall give his angels charge concerning thee to keep thee: and in their hands they shall bear thee up, lest at any time thou dash thy foot against a stone.' " Jesus said unto him, "It is written again, 'Thou shalt not tempt the Lord thy God.' " Again, the devil taketh him up into an exceeding high mountain, and sheweth him all the kingdoms of the world, and the glory of them in a moment of time; and saith unto him, "All this power and all these things will I give thee, and the glory of them; for that is delivered unto me; and to whomsoever I will give it; if thou wilt fall down and worship me, all shall be thine." Then saith Jesus unto him, "Get thee hence, Satan: for it is written, 'Thou shalt worship the Lord thy God, and him only

---

*I have used the account in Matthew for the order of the temptations, with additions from Luke.

shalt thou serve.' " And when the devil had ended all the temptation, he leaveth him [for a season—Luke], and behold angels came and ministered unto him.

JESUS' GENEALOGY*

And Jesus began to be about thirty years of age, being (as was supposed) the son of Joseph, which was *the son* of Heli, which was *the son* of Matthat, which was *the son* of Levi, which was *the son* of Melchi, which was *the son* of Janna, which was *the son* of Joseph, which was *the son* of Mattathias, which was *the son* of Amos, which was *the son* of Naum, which was *the son* of Esli, which was *the son* of Nagge, which was *the son* of Maath, which was *the son* of Mattathias, which was *the son* of Semei, which was *the son* of Joseph, which was *the son* of Juda, which was *the son* of Joanna, which was *the son* of Rhesa, which was *the son* of Zorobabel, which was *the son* of Salathiel, which was *the son* of Neri, which was *the son* of Melchi, which was *the son* of Addi, which was *the son* of Cosam, which was *the son* of Elmodam, which was *the son* of Er, which was *the son* of Jose, which was *the son* of Eliezer, which was *the son* of Jorim, which was *the son* of Matthat, which was *the son* of Levi, which was *the son* of Simeon, which was *the son* of Juda, which was *the son* of Joseph, which was *the son* of Jonan, which was *the son* of Eliakim, which was *the son* of Melea, which was *the son* of Menan, which was *the son* of Mattatha, which was *the son* of Nathan, which was *the son* of David, which was *the son* of Jesse, which was *the son* of Obed, which was *the son* of Booz, which was *the son* of Salmon, which was *the son* of Naasson, which was *the son* of Aminadab, which was *the son* of Aram, which was *the son* of Esrom, which was *the son* of Phares, which was *the son* of Juda, which was *the son* of Jacob, which was *the son*

*I have chosen the genealogy from Luke as the prime source: traditionally that has been taken as the genealogy through Mary, as it avoids the curse of Jeconiah, who appears in Matthew.

of Isaac, which was *the son* of Abraham, which was *the son* of Thara, which was *the son* of Nachor, which was *the son* of Saruch, which was *the son* of Ragau, which was *the son* of Phalec, which was *the son* of Heber, which was *the son* of Sala, which was *the son* of Cainan, which was *the son* of Arphaxad, which was *the son* of Sem, which was *the son* of Noe, which was *the son* of Lamech, which was *the son* of Mathusala, which was *the son* of Enoch, which was *the son* of Jared, which was *the son* of Maleleel, which was *the son* of Cainan, which was *the son* of Enos, which was *the son* of Seth, which was *the son* of Adam, which was *the son* of God. [Matthew traces the descent through Solomon rather than Nathan: David the king begat Solomon of her *that had been the wife* of Urias; and Solomon begat Roboam; and Roboam begat Abia; and Abia begat Asa; and Asa begat Josaphat; and Josaphat begat Joram; and Joram begat Ozias; and Ozias begat Joatham; and Joatham begat Achaz; and Achaz begat Ezekias; and Ezekias begat Manasses; and Manasses begat Amon; and Amon begat Josias; and Josias begat Jechonias and his brethren, about the time they were carried away to Babylon; and after they were brought to Babylon, Jechonias begat Salathiel; and Salathiel begat Zorobabel; and Zorobabel begat Abiud; and Abiud begat Eliakim; and Eliakim begat Azor; and Azor begat Sadoc; and Sadoc begat Achim; and Achim begat Eliud; and Eliud begat Eleazar; and Eleazar begat Matthan; and Matthan begat Jacob; and Jacob begat Joseph the husband of Mary, of whom was born Jesus, who is called Christ. So all the generations from Abraham to David *are* fourteen generations; and from David until the carrying away into Babylon *are* fourteen generations; and from the carrying away into Babylon unto Christ *are* fourteen generations.]

THE CALLING OF THE DISCIPLES

The next day after John stood, and two of his disciples; and looking upon Jesus as he walked, he saith, "Behold the Lamb of

God!" And the two disciples heard him speak, and they followed Jesus. Then Jesus turned and saw them following, and saith unto them, "What seek ye?" They said unto him, "Rabbi, (which is to say, being interpreted, 'Master') where dwellest thou?" He saith unto them, "Come and see." They came and saw where he dwelt, and abode with him that day: for it was about the tenth hour. One of the two which heard John *speak*, and followed him, was Andrew, Simon Peter's brother. He first findeth his own brother Simon, and saith unto him, "We have found the Messias," which is, being interpreted, the Christ. And he brought him to Jesus. And when Jesus beheld him, he said, "Thou art Simon the son of Jona: thou shalt be called Cephas," which is by interpretation, A stone.

The day following Jesus would go forth into Galilee, and findeth Philip, and saith unto him, "Follow me." Now Philip was of Bethsaida, the city of Andrew and Peter. Philip findeth Nathanael, and saith unto him, "We have found him, of whom Moses in the law, and the prophets, did write, Jesus of Nazareth, the son of Joseph." And Nathanael said unto him, "Can there any good thing come out of Nazareth?" Philip saith unto him, "Come and see." Jesus saw Nathanael coming to him, and saith of him, "Behold an Israelite indeed, in whom is no guile!" Nathanael saith unto him, "Whence knowest thou me?" Jesus answered and said unto him, "Before that Philip called thee, when thou wast under the fig tree, I saw thee." Nathanael answered and saith unto him, "Rabbi, thou art the Son of God; thou art the King of Israel." Jesus answered and said unto him, "Because I said unto thee, 'I saw thee under the fig tree,' believest thou? thou shalt see greater things than these." And he saith unto him, "Verily, verily, I say unto you, Hereafter ye shall see heaven open, and the angels of God ascending and descending upon the Son of man."

And leaving Nazareth, he came and dwelt in Capernaum, which is upon the sea coast, in the borders of Zabulon and Nephthalim: that it might be fulfilled which was spoken by Esaias the prophet, saying, "The land of Zabulon and the land of Nephthalim, *by* the way of the sea, beyond Jordan, Galilee of the Gentiles; the people which sat in darkness saw great light; and to them which sat in the region and shadow of death light is sprung up." From that time Jesus began to preach the gospel of the kingdom of God, saying, "The time is fulfilled, and the kingdom of God is at hand; repent ye, and believe the gospel."

Now as he walked by the sea of Galilee [by the lake of Gennesaret—Luke*] the people pressed upon him to hear the word of God.† And he saw two ships standing by the lake; but the fishermen, Simon and Andrew, were gone out of them, and were washing *their* nets. And he entered into one of the ships, which was Simon's, and prayed him that he would thrust out a little from the land. And he sat down, and taught the people out of the ship. Now when he had left speaking, he said unto Simon, "Launch out into the deep, and let down your nets for a draught." And Simon answering said unto him, "Master, we have toiled all the night, and have taken nothing: nevertheless at thy word I will let down the net." And when they had this done, they inclosed a great multitude of fishes: and their net brake. And they beckoned unto *their* partners, which were in the other ship, that they should come and help them. And they came, and filled both the ships, so that they began to sink. When Simon Peter saw *it*, he fell down at Jesus' knees, saying, "Depart from me; for I am a sinful man, O Lord." For he was astonished, and all that were with him, at the draught of the fishes which they had taken. And Jesus said unto Simon *and Andrew*, "Fear not; follow me; from henceforth I will make you to become fishers of men." [thou shalt catch men—Luke] And when they had brought their ships to land, they forsook their nets, and followed him. And when he had gone a little farther hence, he saw other two brethren, James the *son* of Zebedee, and John his brother,

---

*Gennesaret was a coastal town on the Sea of Galilee.

†There is an apparent discrepancy in time between the two calls of Andrew and Simon, but the sequence works out well, as the wording of the second call in no way would contradict their having met before. Indeed, Peter's wording could be taken to infer a previous meeting and relationship.

which were partners with Simon, who also were in the ship mending their nets with Zebedee their father. And straightway he called them, and they left their father Zebedee in the ship with the hired servants, and went after him.

MARRIAGE IN CANA

And the third day there was a marriage in Cana of Galilee; and the mother of Jesus was there: and both Jesus was called, and his disciples, to the marriage. And when they wanted wine, the mother of Jesus saith unto him, "They have no wine." Jesus saith unto her, "Woman, what have I to do with thee? [literally, "what is it between me and thee?"] mine hour is not yet come." His mother saith unto the servants, "Whatsoever he saith unto you, do it." And there were set there six waterpots of stone, after the manner of the purifying of the Jews, containing two or three firkins apiece. Jesus saith unto them, "Fill the waterpots with water." And they filled them up to the brim. And he saith unto them, "Draw out now, and bear unto the governor of the feast." And they bare *it*. When the ruler of the feast had tasted the water that was made wine, and knew not whence it was: (but the servants which drew the water knew;) the governor of the feast called the bridegroom, and saith unto him, "Every man at the beginning doth set forth good wine; and when men have well drunk, then that which is worse: *but* thou hast kept the good wine until now." This beginning of miracles did Jesus in Cana of Galilee, and manifested forth his glory; and his disciples believed on him.

JESUS' FIRST JOURNEY TO JERUSALEM

After this he went down to Capernaum, he, and his mother, and his brethren, and his disciples; and they continued there not many days. And the Jews' passover was at hand, and Jesus went up to Jerusalem.* Now when he was in Jerusalem at the passover, in the feast *day*, many believed in his name, when they saw the miracles which he did. But Jesus did not commit himself unto them, because he knew all men, and needed not that any should testify of man: for he knew what was in man.

THE VISIT OF NICODEMUS

There was a man of the Pharisees, named Nicodemus, a ruler of the Jews: the same came to Jesus by night, and said unto him, "Rabbi, we know that thou art a teacher come from God: for no man can do these miracles that thou doest, except God be with him." Jesus answered and said unto him, "Verily, verily, I say unto thee, Except a man be born again, he cannot see the kingdom of God." Nicodemus saith unto him, "How can a man be born when he is old? can he enter the second time into his mother's womb, and be born?" Jesus answered, "Verily, verily, I say unto thee, Except a man be born of water and of the Spirit, he cannot enter into the kingdom of God. That which is born of the flesh is flesh; and that which is born of the Spirit is spirit. Marvel not that I said unto thee, 'Ye must be born again.' The wind bloweth where it listeth, and thou hearest the sound thereof, but canst not tell whence it cometh, and whither it goeth: so is every one that is born of the Spirit." Nicodemus answered and said unto him, "How can these things be?" Jesus answered and said unto him, "Art thou a master of Israel, and knowest not these things? Verily, verily, I say unto thee, We speak that we do know, and testify that we have seen; and ye receive not our witness. If I have told you earthly things, and ye believe not, how shall ye believe, if I tell you of heavenly things? And no man hath ascended up to heaven, but he that came

*John places the cleansing of the Temple at this point in his narrative, see p. 129.

down from heaven, *even* the Son of man which is in heaven. And as Moses lifted up the serpent in the wilderness, even so must the Son of man be lifted up: that whosoever believeth in him should not perish, but have eternal life. For God so loved the world, that he gave his only begotten Son, that whosoever believeth in him should not perish, but have everlasting life. For God sent not his Son into the world to condemn the world; but that the world through him might be saved. He that believeth on him is not condemned: but he that believeth not is condemned already, because he hath not believed in the name of the only begotten Son of God. And this is the condemnation, that light is come into the world, and men loved darkness rather than light, because their deeds were evil. For every one that doeth evil hateth the light, neither cometh to the light, lest his deeds should be reproved. But he that doeth truth cometh to the light, that his deeds may be made manifest, that they are wrought in God."

JOHN TESTIFIES OF JESUS

After these things came Jesus and his disciples into the land of Judaea; and there he tarried with them, and baptized. And John was also baptizing in Aenon near to Salim, because there was much water there: and they came, and were baptized. For John was not yet cast into prison. Then there arose a question between *some* of John's disciples and the Jews about purifying. And they came unto John and said unto him, "Rabbi, he that was with thee beyond Jordan, to whom thou barest witness, behold, the same baptizeth, and all *men* come to him." John answered and said, "A man can receive nothing, except it be given him from heaven. Ye yourselves bear me witness, that I said, 'I am not the Christ, but that I am sent before him.' He that hath the bride is the bridegroom: but the friend of the bridegroom, which standeth and heareth him, rejoiceth greatly

because of the bridegroom's voice: this my joy therefore is fulfilled. He must increase, but I *must* decrease. He that cometh
from above is above all: he that is of the earth is earthly, and
speaketh of the earth: he that cometh from heaven is above all.
And what he hath seen and heard, that he testifieth; and no
man receiveth his testimony. He that hath received his testimony
hath set to his seal that God is true. For he whom God hath sent
speaketh the words of God: for God giveth not the Spirit by
measure *unto him.* The Father loveth the Son, and hath given all
things into his hand. He that believeth on the Son hath everlasting life: and he that believeth not the Son shall not see life; but
the wrath of God abideth on him.

JOHN'S IMPRISONMENT

But Herod the tetrarch, being reproved by him (John) for Herodias his brother Philip's wife, and for all the evils which Herod
had done, added yet this above all, that he shut up John in prison.
Now when Jesus had heard that John was cast into prison, he left
Judaea, and returned again in the power of the Spirit into Galilee,
for the Lord knew how the Pharisees had heard that Jesus made
and baptized more disciples than John, (Though Jesus himself
baptized not, but his disciples.)

THE WOMAN OF SAMARIA

And he must needs go through Samaria. Then cometh he to a
city of Samaria, which is called Sychar, near to the parcel of
ground that Jacob gave to his son Joseph. Now Jacob's well was
there. Jesus therefore, being wearied with *his* journey, sat thus
on the well: *and* it was about the sixth hour. There cometh a
woman of Samaria to draw water: Jesus saith unto her, "Give

me to drink." (For his disciples were gone away unto the city to buy meat.) Then saith the woman of Samaria unto him, "How is it that thou, being a Jew, askest drink of me, which am a woman of Samaria? for the Jews have no dealings with the Samaritans." Jesus answered and said unto her, "If thou knewest the gift of God, and who it is that saith to thee, 'Give me to drink'; thou wouldest have asked of him, and he would have given thee living water." The woman saith unto him, "Sir, thou hast nothing to draw with, and the well is deep: from whence then hast thou that living water? Art thou greater than our father Jacob, which gave us the well, and drank thereof himself, and his children, and his cattle?" Jesus answered and said unto her, "Whosoever drinketh of this water shall thirst again: but whosoever drinketh of the water that I shall give him shall never thirst: but the water that I shall give him shall be in him a well of water springing up into everlasting life." The woman saith unto him, "Sir, give me this water, that I thirst not, neither come hither to draw."

Jesus saith unto her, "Go, call thy husband, and come hither." The woman answered and said, "I have no husband." Jesus said unto her, "Thou hast well said, 'I have no husband': for thou hast had five husbands; and he whom thou now hast is not thy husband: in that saidst thou truly." The woman saith unto him, "Sir, I perceive that thou art a prophet. Our fathers worshipped in this mountain; and ye say, that in Jerusalem is the place where men ought to worship." Jesus saith unto her, "Woman, believe me, the hour cometh, when ye shall neither in this mountain, nor yet at Jerusalem worship the Father. Ye worship ye know not what: we know what we worship: for salvation is of the Jews. But the hour cometh, and now is, when the true worshippers shall worship the Father in spirit and in truth: for the Father seeketh such to worship him. God *is* a Spirit: and they that worship him must worship *him* in spirit and in truth." The woman saith unto him, "I know that Messias cometh, which is called Christ: when he is come, he will tell us all things." Jesus saith unto her, "I that speak unto thee am *he*."

And upon this came his disciples, and marvelled that he talked with the woman: yet no man said, "What seekest thou?" or, "Why talkest thou with her?" The woman then left her waterpot, and went her way into the city, and saith to the men, "Come, see a man, which told me all things that ever I did: is not this the Christ?" Then they went out of the city, and came unto him.

In the mean while his disciples prayed him, saying, "Master, eat." But he said unto them, "I have meat to eat that ye know not of." Therefore said the disciples one to another, "Hath any man brought him *ought* to eat?" Jesus saith unto them, "My meat is to do the will of him that sent me, and to finish his work. Say not ye, 'There are yet four months, and *then* cometh harvest?' behold, I say unto you, Lift up your eyes, and look on the fields; for they are white already to harvest. And he that reapeth receiveth wages, and gathereth fruit unto life eternal: that both he that soweth and he that reapeth may rejoice together. And herein is that saying true, 'One soweth, and another reapeth.' I sent you to reap that whereon ye bestowed no labour: other men laboured, and ye are entered into their labours."

And many of the Samaritans of that city believed on him for the saying of the woman, which testified, "He told me all that ever I did." So when the Samaritans were come unto him, they besought him that he would tarry with them: and he abode there two days. And many more believed because of his own word; and said unto the woman, "Now we believe, not because of thy saying: for we have heard *him* ourselves, and know that this is indeed the Christ, the Saviour of the world."

PREACHING AND HEALING IN GALILEE

Now after two days he departed thence, and went into Galilee. Then when he was come into Galilee, the Galilaeans received him, having seen all the things that he did at Jerusalem at the

feast: for they also went unto the feast. So Jesus came again into
Cana of Galilee, where he made the water wine. And there was
a certain nobleman, whose son was sick at Capernaum. When
he heard that Jesus was come out of Judaea into Galilee, he went
unto him, and besought him that he would come down, and
heal his son: for he was at the point of death. Then said Jesus
unto him, "Except ye see signs and wonders, ye will not believe."
The nobleman saith unto him, "Sir, come down ere my child
die." Jesus saith unto him, "Go thy way; thy son liveth." And the
man believed the word that Jesus had spoken unto him, and he
went his way. And as he was now going down, his servants met
him, and told *him*, saying, "Thy son liveth." Then enquired he of
them the hour when he began to amend. And they said unto
him, "Yesterday at the seventh hour the fever left him." So the
father knew that *it was* at the same hour, in the which Jesus
said unto him, "Thy son liveth": and himself believed, and his
whole house. This *is* again the second miracle *that* Jesus did,
when he was come out of Judaea into Galilee, and there went
out a fame of him through all the region round about, and he
taught in their synagogues, being glorified of all.

And he came to Nazareth, where he had been brought up:
and, as his custom was, he went into the synagogue on the
sabbath day, and stood up for to read. And there was delivered
unto him the book of the prophet Esaias. And when he had
opened the book, he found the place where it was written, "The
Spirit of the Lord *is* upon me, because he hath anointed me to
preach the gospel to the poor; he hath sent me to heal the
brokenhearted, to preach deliverance to the captives, and re-
covering of sight to the blind, to set at liberty them that are
bruised, to preach the acceptable year of the Lord." And he
closed the book, and he gave *it* again to the minister, and sat
down. And the eyes of all them that were in the synagogue were
fastened on him. And he began to say unto them, "This day is
this scripture fulfilled in your ears." And all bare him witness,
and wondered at the gracious words which proceeded out of his

mouth. And they said, "Is not this Joseph's son?" And he said
unto them, "Ye will surely say unto me this proverb, 'Physician,
heal thyself': whatsoever we have heard done in Capernaum, do
also here in thy country." And he said, "Verily, I say unto you,
No prophet is accepted [hath honour—John] in his own country.
But I tell you of a truth, many widows were in Israel in the days
of Elias, when the heaven was shut up three years and six
months, when great famine was throughout all the land; but
unto none of them was Elias sent, save unto Sarepta, *a city* of
Sidon, unto a woman *that was* a widow. And many lepers were
in Israel in the time of Eliseus the prophet; and none of them
was cleansed, saving Naaman the Syrian." And all they in the
synagogue, when they heard these things, were filled with
wrath, and rose up, and thrust him out of the city, and led him
unto the brow of the hill whereon their city was built, that they
might cast him down headlong. But he passing through the
midst of them went his way.

CASTS OUT AN UNCLEAN SPIRIT

And they went into Capernaum; and straightway on the sabbath
day he entered into the synagogue, and taught. And in the synagogue there was a man, which had a spirit of an unclean devil,
and cried out with a loud voice, saying, "Let *us* alone; what have
we to do with thee, *thou* Jesus of Nazareth? art thou come to
destroy us? I know thee who thou art; the Holy One of God."
And Jesus rebuked him, saying, "Hold thy peace, and come out
of him." And when the devil [unclean spirit—Mark] had thrown
him in the midst, and torn him, and cried with a loud voice, he
came out of him and hurt him not. And they were all amazed,
insomuch that they questioned, and spake among themselves,
saying, "What a word *is* this! What thing is this? what new
doctrine is this? for with authority and power commandeth he

even the unclean spirits, and they do obey him, and they come out." And immediately his fame went out into every place of the country round about Galilee.

JESUS CURES PETER'S MOTHER-IN-LAW

And forthwith, when they arose and were come out of the synagogue, they entered into the house of Simon and Andrew, with James and John. And Simon's wife's mother lay sick with a great fever; and they tell him and besought him for her. And he came and stood over her and took her by the hand, and lifted her up, and rebuked the fever; and immediately the fever left her: and she arose and ministered unto them.

HEALS DIVERSE DISEASES

And at even, when the sun was setting, all they that had any sick with divers diseases, and them that were possessed with devils, brought them unto him. And all the city was gathered together at the door. And he laid his hands on everyone of them, and healed many that were sick of divers diseases, and he cast out the spirits with his word, and many devils came out crying, and saying, "Thou art Christ the Son of God." And he rebuking them suffered them not to speak: for they knew that he was Christ. That it might be fulfilled which was spoken by Esaias the prophet, saying, "Himself took our infirmities, and bare our sicknesses."

And in the morning, rising up a great while before day, he went out and departed into a solitary, desert place, and there prayed. And Simon and the people that were with him followed after him, sought him, found him, and came unto him and stayed him, that he should not depart from them, and said unto him, "All men seek for thee." And he said unto them, "I must preach the kingdom of God to other cities also: for therefore am I sent [came I forth—Mark]." And he said unto them, "Let us go into the next towns, that I may preach there also." And he preached in their synagogues throughout all Galilee, and cast out devils.

And it came to pass when he was in a certain city, behold a man full of leprosy, seeing Jesus, fell on his face and worshipped him, beseeching him, and kneeling down to him, and saying unto him, "Lord, if thou wilt, thou canst make me clean." And Jesus, moved with compassion, put forth *his* hand, and touched him, and saith unto him, "I will; be thou clean." And as soon as he had spoken, immediately the leprosy departed from him, and he was cleansed. And he straitly charged him, and forthwith sent him away; and saith unto him, "See thou say nothing to any man: but go thy way, shew thyself to the priest, and offer for thy cleansing those things which Moses commanded, for a testimony unto them." But he went out, and began to publish *it* much, and to blaze abroad the matter, insomuch that Jesus could no more openly enter into the city, but was without in desert places: and they came to him from every quarter.

HEALING OF THE MAN WITH PALSY

And he entered into a ship, and passed over, and came into his own city [Capernaum—Mark]; and it was noised that he was in the house, teaching, and straightway many were gathered together, insomuch that there was no room to receive *them*, no, not so much as about the door: and he preached the word unto them. And, behold, they brought in a bed a man which was taken sick of the palsy, which was borne of four: and they sought *means* to bring him in, and to lay *him* before him. And when they could not find by what *way* they might bring him in or come nigh unto him because of the press of the multitude, they went upon the housetop, uncovered the roof where he was, and when they had broken it up, they let down the bed wherein the sick of the palsy lay through the tiling into the midst before Jesus. And when he saw their faith, he said unto the sick of the palsy, "Son [Man—Luke], be of good cheer, thy sins are forgiven thee." And the scribes and the Pharisees began to reason within themselves [reasoning in their hearts—Mark], saying, "Who is this *man* which speaketh blasphemies? Who can forgive sins, but God alone?" And immediately when Jesus perceived in his spirit that they so reasoned within themselves, knowing their thoughts, he said unto them, "Why reason ye these evil things in your hearts? For whether is it easier to say to the sick of the palsy, 'Thy sins be forgiven thee'; or to say, 'Arise, and take up thy bed, and walk?' But that ye may know that the Son of man hath power on earth to forgive sins." (then saith he to the sick of the palsy,) "I say unto thee, arise, and take up thy bed, and go thy way into thine house." And immediately he rose up before them, and took up the bed whereon he lay, and went forth before them all, and departed to his own house, glorifying God. And when the multitudes saw it, they were all amazed, and they glorified God, which had given such power unto men, and were filled with fear, saying, "We never saw it on this fashion. We have seen strange things today."

FEAST IN THE HOUSE OF MATTHEW (LEVI)

And after these things he went forth again by the sea side; and all the multitude resorted unto him, and he taught them. And as he passed by, he saw Levi the *son* of Alphaeus,* a publican, sitting at the receipt of custom; and he said unto him, "Follow

---

*Matthew says it was Matthew, and he ought to know. Most critics attribute the event to Matthew.

me." And he left all, rose up, and followed him. And Levi made him a great feast in his own house: and there was a great company of publicans and sinners that sat down with Jesus and his disciples: for there were many, and they followed him. And it came to pass, that, as Jesus sat at meat in his house the scribes and Pharisees saw him eat with publicans and sinners, and they murmured and said unto his disciples, "How is it that he eateth and drinketh with publicans and sinners?" But when Jesus heard *that*, he answered and said unto them, "They that are whole have no need of a physician, but they that are sick. I came not to call the righteous, but sinners to repentance."

NEW WINE IN NEW BOTTLES

And the disciples of John and of the Pharisees used to fast: and they come and say unto him, "Why do the disciples of John and of the Pharisees fast often, and make prayers, but thy disciples fast not: thine eat and drink?" And Jesus said unto them, "Can ye make the children of the bridechamber fast while the bridegroom is with them? as long as they have the bridegroom with them, they cannot fast. But the days will come, when the bridegroom shall be taken away from them, and then shall they fast in those days." And he spake also a parable unto them: "No man seweth a piece of new cloth on an old garment, for that new piece which is put in to fill it up agreeth not with the old and maketh a rent and taketh from the old garment, and the rent is made worse. And no man putteth new wine into old bottles: else the new wine will burst the bottles, and the bottles break and the wine runneth out, and the bottles will be marred and shall perish. But new wine must be put into new bottles, and both are preserved. No man also having drunk old *wine* straightway desireth new; for he saith, 'The old is better.' "

JESUS REPLIES TO HIS CRITICS

And it came to pass that Jesus went through the cornfields on the sabbath [the second sabbath after the first—Luke]; and his disciples were an hungred, and began, as they went, to pluck the ears of corn, and to eat, rubbing *them* in *their* hands. And when certain of the Pharisees saw it, they said unto him [them—Luke], "Behold why do thy disciples do what is not lawful upon the sabbath day?" And Jesus answering them said, "Have ye never read [not read so much as this—Luke] what David did, when he had need, and was an hungred, he, and they that were with him? How he entered into the house of God in the days of Abiathar the high priest, and did take and eat the shewbread, and gave also to them that were with him; which is not lawful for him to eat, neither for them which were with him, but only for the priests? Or have ye not read in the law, how that on the sabbath days the priests in the temple profane the sabbath, and are blameless? But I say unto you, that in this place is *one* greater than the temple. But if ye had known what *this* meaneth, 'I will have mercy, and not sacrifice,' ye would not have condemned the guiltless. The sabbath was made for man, and not man for the sabbath: therefore the Son of man is Lord also of the sabbath."

HEALS MAN WITH WITHERED HAND

And it came to pass also on another sabbath [when he was departed thence—Matthew] that he entered into their synagogue [the house of one of the chief Pharisees to eat bread—Luke] and taught. And, behold, there was a man there whose right hand was withered [had the dropsy—Luke]. And the scribes and Pharisees watch him, whether he would heal him on the sabbath day; that they might find an accusation against him. But he knew their thoughts, and he saith unto them, "I will ask you one thing: is it lawful to heal on the sabbath days? to do good, or to do evil? to save life or to destroy it?" But they held their peace. And he said unto them, "What man shall there be among you, that shall have one sheep, or an ass or an ox, and if it fall into a pit on the sabbath day, will he not straightway lay hold on it, and lift it out? How much then is a man better than a sheep? Wherefore it is lawful to do well on the sabbath days." And they could not answer him again to these things. And he saith unto the man which had the withered hand, "Rise up and stand forth in the midst." And he arose and stood forth. And when he had looked around about on them with anger, being grieved for the hardness of their hearts, he saith unto the man, "Stretch forth thine hand." And he stretched it forth; and his hand was restored whole as the other. And the Pharisees were filled with madness and went forth, and straightway held a council with the Herodians against him, what they might do to destroy him. But when Jesus knew *it*, he withdrew himself with his disciples to the sea; and a great multitude of people [Pharisees and doctors of the law—Luke] from Galilee followed him, and *from* Decapolis, and *from* Jerusalem, and *from* Judaea, and *from* beyond Jordan, and from Idumaea, and he healed them all; and charged them that they should not make him known: that it might be fulfilled which was spoken by Esaias the prophet, saying, "Behold my servant, whom I have chosen; my beloved, in whom my soul is well pleased: I will put my spirit upon him, and he shall shew judgment to the Gentiles. He shall not strive, nor cry; neither shall any man hear his voice in the streets. A bruised reed shall he not break, and smoking flax shall he not quench, till he send forth judgment into victory. And in his name shall the Gentiles trust."*

And Jesus went about all Galilee, teaching in their synagogues, and preaching the gospel of the kingdom, and healing all manner of sickness and all manner of disease among the people. And his fame went throughout all Syria, and they about Tyre

---

*Luke has the multitudes come to him "in the plain" and inserts the "Sermon" immediately following.

and Sidon, a great multitude, when they had heard what great things he did, came unto him to hear him, and to be healed of their diseases, and they brought unto him all sick people that were taken with divers diseases and torments, and those which were possessed with devils, and those which were lunatick, and those that had the palsy; and he healed them all.

And he spake to his disciples, that a small ship should wait on him because of the multitude, lest they should throng him. For there went virtue out of him, and he healed many [all—Luke]; insomuch that they pressed upon him for to touch him, as many as had plagues, and unclean spirits, when they saw him, fell down before him, and cried, saying, "Thou art the Son of God." And he straitly charged them that they should not make him known.

THE CALLING OF THE APOSTLES

And it came to pass in those days, that he went up into a mountain to pray, and continued all night in prayer to God, and when it was day, he called *unto him* his disciples whom he would: and they came unto him. And of them he chose twelve, whom also he named apostles. And he ordained twelve, that they should be with him, and that he might send them forth to preach; and he gave them power *against* unclean spirits [devils—Matthew], to cast them out and to heal all manner of sickness and all manner of disease. Now the names of the twelve apostles are these: the first, Simon (whom he also named Peter,) and Andrew his brother, and James *the son* of Zebedee, and John the brother of James; and he surnamed them Boanerges, which is, "The sons of thunder"; Philip, and Bartholomew, Thomas and Matthew the publican; James *the son* of Alphaeus, and Lebbaeus whose surname was Thaddeus;* Simon the Canaanite called Zelotes, and

*Luke names Judas, the brother of James, in his place.

Judas Iscariot, which also was the traitor who betrayed him: and they went into a house.

SERMON ON THE MOUNT

The Beatitudes

And seeing the multitudes, he went up into a mountain: and when he was set, his disciples came unto him: and he lifted up his eyes on his disciples; and he opened his mouth, and taught them, saying, "Blessed *are* the poor in spirit: for theirs is the kingdom of heaven. Blessed *are* they that mourn: for they shall be comforted. Blessed *are* the meek: for they shall inherit the earth. Blessed *are* they which do hunger and thirst after righteousness now; for they shall be filled. Blessed *are ye* that weep now: for ye shall laugh. Blessed *are* the merciful: for they shall obtain mercy. Blessed *are* the pure in heart: for they shall see God. Blessed *are* the peace-makers: for they shall be called the children of God. Blessed *are* they which are persecuted for righteousness' sake: for theirs is the kingdom of heaven. Blessed are ye, when men shall hate you and revile you, and persecute you, and when they shall separate you *from their company*, and shall reproach *you*, and shall say all manner of evil against you falsely, and cast out your name as evil, for my [the Son of man's—Luke] sake. Rejoice ye in that day, and be exceeding glad, and leap for joy: for, behold your reward *is* great in heaven: for in the like manner persecuted their fathers the prophets which were before you. But woe unto you that are rich! for ye have received your consolation. Woe unto you that are full! for ye shall hunger. Woe unto you that laugh now! for ye shall mourn and weep. Woe unto you, when all men shall speak well of you! for so did their fathers to the false prophets.

"Ye are the salt of the earth: salt is good: but if the salt have lost his savour, wherewith shall it be salted? it is thenceforth good for nothing, neither for the land, nor yet the dunghill; but to be cast out, and to be trodden underfoot of men. He who hath ears to hear, let him hear. Ye are the light of the world. A city that is set on an hill cannot be hid. Neither do men light a candle, and put it in a secret place, neither under a bushel, but on a candlestick; and it giveth light unto all that are in the house. Let your light so shine before men, that they may see your good works, and glorify your Father which is in heaven.

RESTATEMENT OF THE LAW

"The law and the prophets *were* until John: since that time the kingdom of God is preached, and every man presseth into it. Think not that I am come to destroy the law, or the prophets: I am not come to destroy, but to fulfill. For verily I say unto you, Till heaven and earth pass, one jot or one tittle shall in no wise pass from the law, till all be fulfilled. Whosoever therefore shall break one of these least commandments, and shall teach men so, he shall be called the least in the kingdom of heaven: but whosoever shall do and teach *them*, the same shall be called great in the kingdom of heaven. For I say unto you, That except your righteousness shall exceed *the righteousness* of the scribes and Pharisees, ye shall in no case enter into the kingdom of heaven. Ye have heard that it was said by them of old time, 'Thou shalt not kill'; and 'Whosoever shall kill shall be in danger of the judgment': but I say unto you, That whosoever is angry with his brother without a cause shall be in danger of the judgment: and whosoever shall say to his brother, 'Raca,' shall be in danger of the council: but whosoever shall say, 'Thou fool,' shall be in danger of hell fire. Therefore if thou bring thy gift to the altar, and there rememberest that thy brother hath ought against thee: leave there thy gift before the altar, and go thy way; first be reconciled to thy brother, and then come and offer thy gift. When thou goest with thine adversary to the magistrate, agree with thine adversary quickly, whiles thou art in the way with him; give diligence that thou mayest be delivered from him, lest at any time the adversary deliver [hale—Luke] thee to the judge, and the judge deliver thee to the officer, and the officer cast thee into prison. Verily I say unto thee, Thou shalt by no means come out thence, till thou hast paid the uttermost farthing [mite—Luke].

"Ye have heard that it was said by them of old time, 'Thou shalt not commit adultery'; but I say unto you, That whosoever looketh on a woman to lust after her hath committed adultery with her already in his heart. And if thy right eye offend thee, pluck it out, and cast *it* from thee: for it is profitable for thee that one of thy members should perish, and not *that* thy whole body should be cast into hell. And if thy right hand offend thee, cut it off, and cast *it* from thee: for it is profitable for thee that one of the members should perish, and not *that* thy whole body should be cast into hell.*

INJUNCTION AGAINST DIVORCE, SWEARING, AND REVENGE

"It hath been said, 'Whosoever shall put away his wife, let him give her a writing of divorcement'; but I say unto you, That whosoever shall put away his wife, saving for the cause of fornication, and marrieth another, committeth adultery and causeth her to commit adultery: and whosoever shall marry her that is divorced committeth adultery. Again, ye have heard that it hath been said by them of old time, 'Thou shalt not forswear thyself, but shalt perform unto the Lord thine oaths': but I say unto you, Swear not at all; neither by heaven; for it is God's throne: nor by the earth; for it is his footstool: neither by Jerusalem; for it is the city of the great King. Neither shalt thou swear by thy head, because thou canst not make one hair white or black. But let

---

*This passage is repeated later (pp. 97–98) but both incidents read as true in context.

your communication be, 'Yea, yea; Nay, nay': for whatsoever is more than these cometh of evil. Ye have heard that it hath been said, 'An eye for an eye, and a tooth for a tooth': but I say unto you, That ye resist not evil: but whosoever shall smite thee on thy right cheek, turn to him the other also. And if any man will sue thee at the law, and take away thy coat, let him have *thy* cloak also. And whosoever shall compel thee to go a mile, go with him twain.

LOVE YOUR ENEMY

"Give to every man that asketh of thee, and from him that would borrow of thee turn not thou away, and of him that taketh away thy goods ask *them* not again. Ye have heard that it hath been said, 'Thou shalt love thy neighbour, and hate thine enemy.' But I say unto you which hear, Love your enemies, bless them that curse you, do good to them that hate you, and lend, hoping for nothing again, and pray for them which despitefully use you, and persecute you; and your reward shall be great; that ye may be the children of your Father which is in heaven, the Highest; for he is kind unto the unthankful and to the evil; for he maketh his sun to rise on the evil and on the good, and sendeth rain on the just and on the unjust. For if ye love them which love you, what reward have ye? do not even the publicans and sinners also love those that love them? And if ye do good to them which do good to you, what thank have ye? for sinners also do even the same. And if ye lend *to them* of whom ye hope to receive, what thank have ye? For sinners also lend to sinners, to receive as much again. And if ye salute your brethren only, what do ye more *than others?* do not even the publicans so? Be ye therefore merciful as your Father also is merciful; be ye therefore perfect, even as your Father which is in heaven is perfect.

ON PRAYER

"Take heed that ye do not your alms before men, to be seen of them: otherwise ye have no reward of your Father which is in heaven. Therefore when thou doest *thine* alms, do not sound a trumpet before thee, as the hypocrites do in the synagogues and in the streets, that they may have glory of men. Verily I say unto you, They have their reward. But when thou doest alms, let not thy left hand know what thy right hand doeth: that thine alms may be in secret; and thy Father which seeth in secret himself shall reward thee openly. And when thou prayest, thou shalt not be as the hypocrites *are:* for they love to pray standing in the synagogues and in the corners of the streets, that they may be seen of men. Verily I say unto you, They have their reward. But thou, when thou prayest, enter into thy closet, and when thou hast shut thy door, pray to thy Father which is in secret; and thy Father which seeth in secret shall reward thee openly. But when ye pray, use not vain repetitions, as the heathen *do:* for they think that they shall be heard for their much speaking. Be not ye therefore like unto them: for your Father knoweth what things ye have need of, before ye ask him."

THE LORD'S PRAYER

One of his disciples said unto him, "Lord, teach us to pray, as John also taught his disciples."* And he said unto them, "When ye pray, after this manner pray ye: 'Our Father which art in heaven, Hallowed be thy name. Thy kingdom come. Thy will be done in earth, as *it is* in heaven. Give us this day [day by day— Luke] our daily bread. And forgive us our debts [sins—Luke], as we forgive our debtors [for we also forgive everyone that is

*Luke places Jesus' teaching of prayer after a time of his own praying.

indebted to us—Luke]. And lead us not into temptation, but deliver us from evil: for thine is the kingdom, and the power, and the glory, for ever. Amen.' For if ye forgive men their trespasses, your heavenly Father will also forgive you: but if ye forgive not men their trespasses, neither will your Father which is in heaven forgive your trespasses. Moreover when ye fast, be not, as the hypocrites, of a sad countenance: for they disfigure their faces, that they may appear unto men to fast. Verily I say unto you, They have their reward. But thou, when thou fastest, anoint thine head, and wash thy face; that thou appear not unto men to fast, but unto thy Father which is in secret: and thy Father, which seeth in secret, shall reward thee openly.

TAKE NO CARE FOR THE FUTURE

"Lay not up for yourselves treasures upon earth, where moth and rust doth corrupt, and where thieves break through and steal: but lay up for yourselves treasures in heaven, where neither moth nor rust doth corrupt, and where thieves do not break through nor steal: for where your treasure is, there will your heart be also. The light of the body is the eye: if therefore thine eye be single, thy whole body shall be full of light. Take heed therefore that the light which is in thee be not darkness. If thy whole body therefore *be* full of light, having no part dark, the whole shall be full of light, as when the bright shining of a candle doth give thee light. But if thine eye be evil, thy whole body shall be full of darkness. If therefore the light that is in thee be darkness, how great *is* that darkness!

"No servant can serve two masters: for either he will hate the one, and love the other; or else he will hold to the one, and despise the other. Ye cannot serve God and mammon. Therefore I say unto you, Take no thought for your life, what ye shall eat, or what ye shall drink; nor yet for your body, what ye shall put on. Is not the life more than meat, and body than raiment?

Behold the fowls of the air [ravens—Luke]: for they sow not, neither do they reap, nor gather into storehouse nor barns; yet your heavenly Father feedeth them. Are ye not much better than the fowls? Which of you by taking thought can add one cubit unto his stature? If ye then be not able to do that thing which is least, why take ye thought for the rest? And why take ye thought for raiment? Consider the lilies of the field, how they grow; they toil not, neither do they spin: and yet I say unto you, That even Solomon in all his glory was not arrayed like one of these. Wherefore, if God so clothe the grass of the field, which to day is, and tomorrow is cast into the oven, *shall he* not much more *clothe* you, O ye of little faith? Therefore take no thought, saying, 'What shall we eat?' or, 'What shall we drink?' or, 'Wherewithal shall we be clothed?' (For after all these things do the Gentiles [nations—Luke] seek.) neither be ye of doubtful mind, for your heavenly Father knoweth that ye have need of all these things. But seek ye first the kingdom of God, and his righteousness; and all these things shall be added unto you. Take therefore no thought for the morrow: for the morrow shall take thought for the things of itself. Sufficient unto the day *is* the evil thereof.

AGAINST JUDGING OTHERS

"Judge not, that ye be not judged; condemn not, and ye shall not be condemned: forgive, and ye shall be forgiven: give, and it shall be given unto you; good measure, pressed down, and shaken together, and running over, shall men give unto your bosom. For with what judgment ye judge, ye shall be judged: and with the same measure that ye mete withal, it shall be measured to you again."

And he spake a parable unto them, "Can the blind lead the blind? shall they not both fall into the ditch? The disciple is not above his master: but every one that is perfect shall be as his master. And why beholdest thou the mote that is in thy brother's eye, but considerest not the beam that is in thine own eye? Or how canst thou say to thy brother, 'Brother, let me pull out the mote that is in thine eye.' when thou thyself beholdest not the beam that is in thine own eye? Thou hypocrite, first cast out the beam out of thine own eye; and then shalt thou see clearly to pull out the mote out of thy brother's eye.

"Give not that which is holy unto the dogs, neither cast ye your pearls before swine, lest they trample them under their feet, and turn again and rend you."

ASK AND IT SHALL BE GIVEN

And he said unto them, "Which of you shall have a friend, and shall go unto him at midnight, and say unto him, 'Friend, lend me three loaves; for a friend of mine in his journey is come to me, and I have nothing to set before him'? And he from within shall answer and say, 'Trouble me not: the door is now shut, and my children are with me in bed; I cannot rise and give thee.' I say unto you, Though he will not rise and give him, because he is his friend, yet because of his importunity he will rise and give him as many as he needeth. And I say unto you, Ask, and it shall be given you; seek, and ye shall find; knock, and it shall be opened unto you: for every one that asketh receiveth; and he that seeketh findeth; and to him that knocketh it shall be opened. Or what man is there of you that is a father, whom if his son ask bread, will he give him a stone? or if he ask a fish, will he for a fish give him a serpent? or if he shall ask an egg, will he offer him a scorpion? If ye then, being evil, know how to give good gifts unto your children, how much more shall your Father which is in heaven give good things [the Holy Spirit—Luke] to them that ask him? Therefore all things whatsoever ye would that man should do to you, do ye even so to them: for this is the law and the prophets.

Enter ye in at the strait gate: for wide is the gate, and broad *is* the way, that leadeth to destruction, and many there be which go in thereat: because strait *is* the gate, and narrow *is* the way, which leadeth unto life, and few there be that find it. Beware of false prophets, which come to you in sheep's clothing, but inwardly they are ravening wolves.

BY THEIR FRUITS SHALL YE KNOW THEM

"Ye shall know them by their fruits, for every tree is known by his own fruit. Do men gather grapes [figs—Luke] of thorns or figs [grapes—Luke] of thistles [a bramble bush—Luke]? Even so every good tree bringeth forth good fruit; but a corrupt tree bringeth forth evil fruit. A good tree cannot bring forth evil fruit, neither *can* a corrupt tree bring forth good fruit. Every tree that bringeth not forth good fruit is hewn down, and cast into the fire. A good man out of the good treasure of his heart bringeth forth that which is good; and an evil man out of the evil treasure of his heart bringeth forth that which is evil: for of the abundance of the heart his mouth speaketh. Wherefore by their fruits ye shall know them.

"And why call ye me, 'Lord, Lord,' and do not the things which I say? Not every one that saith unto me, 'Lord, Lord,' shall enter into the kingdom of heaven; but he that doeth the will of my Father which is in heaven. Many will say to me in that day, 'Lord, Lord, have we not prophesied in thy name? and in thy name have cast out devils? and in thy name done many wonderful works? And then will I profess unto them, 'I never knew you: depart from me, ye that work iniquity.'

HOUSE BUILT ON ROCK

"Therefore whosoever cometh to me, and heareth my sayings, and doeth them, I will shew you to whom he is like: he is like a wise man which built an house, and digged deep, and laid the foundation on a rock: and the rain descended, and the floods arose, and the winds blew, and the stream beat vehemently upon that house, and could not shake it, and it fell not: for it was founded upon a rock. But every one that heareth these sayings of mine, and doeth them not, shall be likened unto a foolish man that without a foundation built his house upon the sand: and the rain descended, and the floods came, and the winds blew, and the stream did beat vehemently upon that house: and immediately it fell: and great was the fall of it."

And it came to pass, when Jesus had ended these sayings, the people were astonished at his doctrine: for he taught them as *one* having authority, and not as the scribes, for his word was with power.

A HOUSE DIVIDED AGAINST ITSELF

And the multitude cometh together again, so that they could not so much as eat bread. And when his friends heard *of it*, they went out to lay hold on him: for they said, "He is beside himself." Then was brought unto him one possessed with a devil, blind, and dumb: and he healed him, insomuch that the blind and dumb both spake and saw. And all the people were amazed and wondered, saying, "It was never so seen in Israel. Is this not the son of David?" And the scribes and Pharisees which came down from Jerusalem heard it, *and* said, "This *fellow* hath Beelzebub, and by the prince of the devils casteth he out devils." And Jesus knew their thoughts, and he called them *unto him*, and said unto them in parables, "How can Satan cast out Satan? And if a kingdom be divided against itself, that kingdom cannot stand *and* is brought to desolation. And if a city or house be divided against itself, it cannot stand and falleth. And if Satan rise up and be divided against himself, and cast out Satan, his kingdom cannot stand, but hath an end, because ye say that I cast out devils through Beelzebub. And if I by Beelzebub cast out devils, by whom do your children cast *them* out? therefore they shall be your judges. But if I cast out devils by the finger [Spirit—Matthew] of God, then no doubt the kingdom of God is come unto you. When a stong man armed keepeth his place, his goods are in peace; no man can enter and spoil his goods. But when a stronger than he shall come upon him and overcome him and bind the strong man, he taketh from him all his armour wherein he trusteth, and then he will spoil his house and divide his spoils.

THE UNFORGIVEABLE SIN

"Verily I say unto you, All sins shall be forgiven unto the sons of men, and blasphemies wherewith soever they shall blaspheme: but he that shall blaspheme against the Holy Ghost hath never forgiveness, but is in danger of eternal damnation": because they said, "He hath an unclean spirit." "And whosoever speaketh a word against the Son of man, it shall be forgiven him: but whosoever speaketh [blasphemeth—Luke] against the Holy Ghost, it shall not be forgiven him, neither in this world, neither in the *world* to come. Either make the tree good, and his fruit good; or else make the tree corrupt, and his fruit corrupt: for the tree is known by *his* fruit.* O generation of vipers, how can ye, being evil, speak good things? But I say unto you, That every idle word that men shall speak, they shall give account thereof in the day of judgment. For by thy words thou shalt be justified, and by thy words thou shalt be condemned. He that is not with me is against me: and he that gathereth not with me scattereth abroad.† When the unclean spirit is gone out of a man, he

---

*This may be a restatement of the similar point on p. 45 rather than a second incident.

†See a parallel statement on p. 100.

walketh through dry places, seeking rest; and finding none, he saith, 'I will return unto my house whence I came out.' And when he cometh, he findeth it empty, swept and garnished. Then goeth he, and taketh with himself seven other spirits more wicked then himself; and they enter in, and dwell there: and the last *state* of that man is worse than the first. Even so shall it be also unto this wicked generation."

THE SIGN OF NOAH

And it came to pass, as he spake these things, a certain woman of the company lifted up her voice, and said unto him, "Blessed *is* the womb that bare thee, and the paps which thou hast sucked." But he said, "Yea rather, blessed *are* they that hear the word of God, and keep it." And when the people were gathered thick together, certain of the scribes and of the Pharisees answered, saying, "Master we would see a sign from heaven from thee," tempting him. But he sighed deeply in his spirit and answered and said unto them, "Why doth this generation seek after a sign? This is an evil and adulterous generation: they seek a sign; and there shall be no sign given it, but the sign of Jonas the prophet. For as Jonas was three days and three nights in the whale's belly; so shall the Son of man be three days and three nights in the heart of the earth. For as Jonas was a sign unto the Ninevites, so shall also the Son of man be to this generation. The men of Nineveh shall rise up in the judgment with this genera-tion, and shall condemn it: for they repented at the preaching of Jonas; and, behold, a greater than Jonah is here. The queen of the south shall rise up in the judgment with the men of this generation, and condemn them; for she came from the utmost parts of the earth to hear the wisdom of Solomon; and, behold, a greater than Solomon *is* here."

HEALING THE CENTURION'S SERVANT

Now when he had ended all his sayings in the audience of the people, he entered into Capernaum. And a certain centurion's servant, who was dear unto him, was sick, and ready to die. And when he heard of Jesus, he sent unto him the elders of the Jews, beseeching him that he would come and heal his servant, saying, "Lord, my servant lieth at home sick of the palsy, grievously tormented." And when they came to Jesus, they besought him instantly, saying, "That he was worthy for whom he should do this: for he loveth our nation, and he hath built us a synagogue." And Jesus saith, "I will come and heal him." Then Jesus went with them. And when he was now not far from the house, the centurion sent friends to him, saying unto him, "Lord, trouble not thyself: for I am not worthy that thou shouldest enter under my roof: wherefore neither thought I myself worthy to come unto thee: but speak the word only, and my servant shall be healed. For I also am a man set under authority, having under me soldiers, and I say unto one, 'Go,' and he goeth: and to another, 'Come,' and he cometh; and to my servant, 'Do this,' and he doeth *it*." When Jesus heard *it*, he marvelled, and turned him about and said to them that followed, "Verily I say unto you, I have not found so great faith, no, not in Israel. And I say unto you, that many shall come from the east and west, and shall sit down with Abraham, and Isaac, and Jacob, in the kingdom of heaven. But the children of the kingdom shall be cast out into outer darkness: there shall be weeping and gnashing of teeth." And Jesus said unto the centurion, "Go thy way; and as thou hast believed, *so* be it done unto thee." And they that were sent, returning to the house, found the servant whole that had been sick. And his servant was healed in the selfsame hour.

RAISES THE WIDOW'S SON

And it came to pass the day after, that he went into a city called Nain; and many of his disciples went with him, and much people. Now when he came nigh to the gate of the city, behold, there was a dead man carried out, the only son of his mother, and she was a widow; and much people of the city was with her. And when the Lord saw her, he had compassion on her, and said unto her, "Weep not." And he came and touched the bier: and they that bare *him* stood still. And he said, "Young man, I say unto thee, Arise." And he that was dead sat up, and began to speak. And he delivered him to his mother. And there came a fear on all: and they glorified God, saying, "That a great prophet is risen up among us; and, That God hath visited his people." And this rumour of him went forth throughout all Judaea, and throughout all the region round about.

JESUS AND JOHN'S DISCIPLES

And the disciples of John shewed him in the prison all these works of Christ. And John calling *unto him* two of his disciples sent *them* to Jesus, saying, "Art thou he that should come? or look we for another?" When the men were come unto him, they said, "John Baptist hath sent us unto thee, saying, 'Art thou he that should come? or look we for another?'" And in that same hour he cured many of *their* infirmities and plagues, and of evil spirits; and unto many *that were* blind he gave sight. Then Jesus answering said unto them, "Go your way, and tell John what things ye have seen and heard: how that the blind receive their sight, the lame walk, the lepers are cleansed, and the deaf hear, the dead are raised, to the poor the gospel is preached. And blessed is *he*, whosoever shall not be offended in me."

And when the messengers of John were departed, he began to speak unto the people concerning John, "What went ye out into the wilderness for to see? A reed shaken with the wind? But what went ye out for to see? A man clothed in soft raiment? Behold, they which are gorgeously apparelled, and live delicately, are in kings' courts. But what went ye out for to see? A prophet? Yea, I say unto you, and much more than a prophet. This is *he*, of whom it is written, 'Behold, I send my messenger before thy face, which shall prepare thy way before thee.' And from the days of John the Baptist until now the kingdom of heaven suffereth violence, and the violent take it by force. For all the prophets and the law prophesied until John. And if ye will receive *it*, this is Elias, which was for to come. He that hath ears to hear, let him hear. For I say unto you, among those that are born of women there is not a greater prophet than John the Baptist: not withstanding, he that is least in the kingdom of God is greater then he." And all the people that heard *him*, and the publicans, justified God, being baptized with the baptism of John. But the Pharisees and lawyers rejected the counsel of God against themselves, being not baptized of him.

And the Lord said, "Whereunto then shall I liken the men of this generation? and to what are they like? They are like unto children sitting in the marketplace, and calling one to another, and saying, "We have piped unto you, and ye have not danced; we have mourned to you, and ye have not wept [lamented— Matthew]." For John the Baptist came neither eating bread nor drinking wine; and ye say, 'He hath a devil.' The Son of man is come eating and drinking; and ye say, 'Behold a gluttonous man, and a winebibber, a friend of publicans and sinners!' But wisdom is justified of all her children."

Then began he to upbraid the cities wherein most of his mighty works were done, because they repented not: "Woe unto thee, Chorazin! woe unto thee, Bethsaida! for if the mighty works, which were done in you, had been done in Tyre and Sidon, they would have repented long ago sitting in sackcloth and ashes. But I say unto you, It shall be more tolerable for Tyre and Sidon at the day of judgment, than for you. And thou Capernaum, which art exalted unto heaven, shalt be brought down to hell: for if the mighty works, which have been done in thee, had been done in Sodom it would have remained until this day. But I say unto you, That it shall be more tolerable for the land of Sodom, in the day of judgment, than for thee."

HIS YOKE IS EASY

At that time Jesus answered and said, "I thank thee, O Father, Lord of heaven and earth, because thou hast hid these things from the wise and prudent, and hast revealed them unto babes. Even so, Father: for so it seemed good in thy sight. All things are delivered unto me of my Father: and no man knoweth the Son, but the Father; neither knoweth any man the Father, save the Son, and *he* to whomsoever the Son will reveal *him*. Come unto me, all *ye* that labour and are heavy laden, and I will give you rest. Take my yoke upon you, and learn of me; for I am meek and lowly in heart: and ye shall find rest unto your souls. For my yoke is easy, and my burden is light."

A WOMAN ANOINTS HIS FEET

And one of the Pharisees desired him that he would eat with him. And he went into the Pharisee's house, and sat down to meat. And, behold, a woman in the city, which was a sinner, when she knew that *Jesus* sat at meat in the Pharisee's house, brought an alabaster box of ointment, and stood at his feet behind him weeping, and began to wash his feet with tears, and did wipe *them* with the hairs of her head, and kissed his feet, and anointed *them* with the ointment.* Now when the Pharisee

*For a parallel event involving Mary, the sister of Lazarus, see pp. 147–148.

which had bidden him saw *it*, he spake within himself, saying, "This man, if he were a prophet, would have known who and what manner of woman *this is* that toucheth him: for she is a sinner." And Jesus answering said unto him, "Simon, I have somewhat to say unto thee." And he saith, "Master, say on." "There was a certain creditor which had two debtors: the one owed five hundred pence, and the other fifty. And when they had nothing to pay, he frankly forgave them both. Tell me therefore, which of them will love him most." Simon answered and said, "I suppose *he*, to whom he forgave most." And he said unto him, "Thou hast rightly judged." And he turned to the woman, and said unto Simon, "Seest thou this woman? I entered into thine house, thou gavest me no water for my feet: but she hath washed my feet with tears, and wiped *them* with the hairs of her head. Thou gavest me no kiss: but this woman since the time I came in hath not ceased to kiss my feet. My head with oil thou didst not anoint: but this woman hath anointed my feet with ointment. Wherefore I say unto thee, Her sins, which are many, are forgiven; for she loved much: but to whom little is forgiven, *the same* loveth little." And he said unto her, "Thy sins are forgiven." And they that sat at meat with him began to say within themselves, "Who is this that forgiveth sins also?" And he said to the woman, "Thy faith hath saved thee; go in peace."

HEALING OF AN INFIRM MAN

After this there was a feast of the Jews; and Jesus went up to Jerusalem. Now there is at Jerusalem by the sheep *market* a pool, which is called in the Hebrew tongue Bethesda, having five porches. In these lay a great multitude of impotent folk, of blind, halt, withered, waiting for the moving of the water. For an angel went down at a certain season into the pool, and troubled the water: whosoever then first after the troubling of the water stepped in was made whole of whatsoever disease he had. And a certain man was there, which had an infirmity thirty and eight years. When Jesus saw him lie, and knew that he had been now a long time *in that case*, he saith unto him, "Wilt thou be made whole?" The impotent men answered him, "Sir, I have no man, when the water is troubled, to put me into the pool: but while I am coming, another steppeth down before me." Jesus saith unto him, "Rise, take up thy bed, and walk." And immediately the man was made whole, and took up his bed, and walked: and on the same day was the sabbath. The Jews therefore said unto him that was cured, "It is the sabbath day: it is not lawful for thee to *carry thy* bed." He answered them, "He that made me whole, the same said unto me, "Take up thy bed, and walk." Then asked they him, "What man is that which said unto thee, 'Take up thy bed, and walk?' " And he that was healed wist not who it was: for Jesus had conveyed himself away, a multitude being in *that* place. Afterward Jesus findeth him in the temple, and said unto him, "Behold, thou art made whole: sin no more, lest a worse thing come unto thee." The man departed, and told the Jews that it was Jesus, which had made him whole. And therefore did the Jews persecute Jesus, and sought to slay him, because he had done these things on the sabbath day. But Jesus answered them, "My Father worketh hitherto, and I work." Therefore the Jews sought the more to kill him, because he not only had broken the sabbath, but said also that God was his Father, making himself equal with God.

THE FATHER'S WITNESS OF THE SON

Then answered Jesus and said unto them, "Verily, verily, I say unto you, the Son can do nothing of himself, but what he seeth the Father do: for what things soever he doeth, these also doeth the Son likewise. For the Father loveth the Son, and sheweth him

all things that himself doeth: and he will shew him greater
works than these, that ye may marvel. For as the Father raiseth
up the dead, and quickeneth *them;* even so the Son quickeneth
whom he will. For the Father judgeth no man, but hath committed all judgment unto the Son: that all *men* should honour
the Son, even as they honour the Father. He that honoureth not
the Son honoureth not the Father which hath sent him. Verily,
verily, I say unto you, He that heareth my word, and believeth
on him that sent me, hath everlasting life, and shall not come
into condemnation; but is passed from death unto life. Verily,
verily, I say unto you, The hour is coming, and now is, when the
dead shall hear the voice of the Son of God: and they that hear
shall live. For as the Father hath life in himself; so hath he given
to the Son to have life in himself; and hath given him authority
to execute judgment also, because he is the Son of man. Marvel
not at this: for the hour is coming, in the which all that are in
the graves shall hear his voice, and shall come forth; they that
have done good, unto the resurrection of life; and they that have
done evil, unto the resurrection of damnation. I can of mine
own self do nothing: as I hear, I judge: and my judgment is just;
because I seek not mine own will, but the will of the Father
which hath sent me. If I bear witness of myself, my witness is
not true. There is another that beareth witness of me; and I
know that the witness which he witnesseth of me is true. Ye sent
unto John, and he bare witness unto the truth. But I receive not
testimony from man: but these things I say, that ye might be
saved. He was a burning and a shining light: and ye were
willing for a season to rejoice in his light. But I have greater
witness than *that* of John: for the works which the Father hath
given me to finish, the same works that I do, bear witness of
me, that the Father hath sent me. And the Father himself,
which hath sent me, hath borne witness of me. Ye have neither
heard his voice at any time, nor seen his shape. And ye have not
his word abiding in you: for whom he hath sent, him ye believe
not."

"SEARCH THE SCRIPTURES"

"Search the scriptures; for in them ye think ye have eternal life: and they are they which testify of me. And ye will not come to me, that ye might have life. I receive not honour from men. But I know you, that ye have not the love of God in you. I am come in my Father's name, and ye receive me not: if another shall come in his own name, him ye will receive. How can ye believe, which receive honour one of another, and seek not the honour that *cometh* from God only? Do not think that I will accuse you to the Father: there is *one* that accuseth you, *even* Moses, in whom ye trust. For had ye believed Moses, ye would have believed me: for he wrote of me. But if ye believe not his writings, how shall ye believe my words?"

THE FEAST OF TABERNACLES

After these things Jesus walked in Galilee: for he would not walk in Jewry, because the Jews sought to kill him. Now the Jews' feast of tabernacles was at hand. His brethren therefore said unto him, "Depart hence, and go into Judaea, that thy disciples also may see the works that thou doest. For *there is* no man *that* doeth any thing in secret, and he himself seeketh to be known openly. If thou do these things, shew thyself to the world." For neither did his brethren believe in him. Then Jesus said unto them, "My time is not yet come: but your time is alway ready. The world cannot hate you; but me it hateth, because I testify of it, that the works thereof are evil. Go ye up unto this feast: I go not up yet unto this feast; for my time is not yet full come." When he had said these words unto them, he abode *still* in Galilee.

But when his brethren were gone up, then went he also up unto the feast, not openly, but as it were in secret. Then the Jews sought him at the feast, and said, "Where is he?" And there was much murmuring among the people concerning him: for some said, "He is a good man": others said, "Nay; but he deceiveth the people." Howbeit no man spake openly of him for fear of the Jews.

TEACHES IN THE TEMPLE

Now about the midst of the feast Jesus went up into the temple, and taught. And the Jews marvelled, saying, "How knoweth this man letters, having never learned?" Jesus answered them, and said, "My doctrine is not mine, but his that sent me. If any man will do his will, he shall know of the doctrine, whether it be of God, or *whether* I speak of myself. He that speaketh of himself seeketh his own glory: but he that seeketh his glory that sent him, the same is true, and no unrighteousness is in him. Did not Moses give you the law, and yet none of you keepeth the law? Why go ye about to kill me?" The people answered and said, "Thou hast a devil: who goeth about to kill thee?" Jesus answered and said unto them, "I have done one work, and ye all marvel. Moses therefore gave unto you circumcision; (not because it is of Moses, but of the fathers;) and ye on the sabbath day circumcise a man. If a man on the sabbath day receive circumcision, that the law of Moses should not be broken; are ye angry at me, because I have made a man every whit whole on the sabbath day? Judge not according to the appearance, but judge righteous judgment." Then said some of them of Jerusalem, "Is not this he, whom they seek to kill? But, lo, he speaketh boldly, and they say nothing unto him. Do the rulers know indeed that this is the very Christ? Howbeit we know this man whence he is: but when Christ cometh, no man knoweth whence he is."

Then cried Jesus in the temple as he taught, saying, "Ye both know me, and ye know whence I am: and I am not come of myself, but he that sent me is true, whom ye know not. But I know him: for I am from him, and he hath sent me." Then they sought to take him: but no man laid hands on him, because his hour was not yet come. And many of the people believed on him, and said, "When Christ cometh, will he do more miracles than these which this *man* hath done?"

The Pharisees heard that the people murmured such things concerning him; and the Pharisees and the chief priests sent officers to take him. Then said Jesus unto them, "Yet a little while am I with you, and *then* I go unto him that sent me. Ye shall seek me, and shall not find *me:* and where I am, *thither* ye cannot come."* Then said the Jews among themselves, "Whither will he go, that we shall not find him? will he go unto the dispersed among the Gentiles, and teach the Gentiles? What *manner of* saying is this that he said, 'Ye shall seek me, and shall not find *me*': and 'where I am, *thither* ye cannot come?' "

In the last day, that great *day* of the feast, Jesus stood and cried, saying, "If any man thirst, let him come unto me, and drink. He that believeth on me, as the scripture hath said, 'out of his belly shall flow rivers of living water.' " (But this spake he of the Spirit, which they that believe on him should receive: for the Holy Ghost was not yet *given;* because that Jesus was not yet glorified.) Many of the people therefore, when they heard this saying, said, "Of a truth this is the Prophet." Others said, "This is the Christ." But some said, "Shall Christ come out of Galilee? Hath not the scripture said, That Christ cometh of the seed of David, and out of the town of Bethlehem, where David was?" So there was a division among the people because of him. And some of them would have taken him; but no man laid hands on him.

Then came the officers to the chief priests and Pharisees; and they said unto them, "Why have ye not brought him?" The

*For a similar statement, see his final speech to his disciples on p. 152.

officers answered, "Never man spake like this man." Then answered them the Pharisees, "Are ye also deceived? Have any of the rulers or of the Pharisees believed on him? But this people who knoweth not the law are cursed." Nicodemus saith unto them, (he that came to Jesus by night, being one of them,) "Doth our law judge *any* man, before it hear him, and know what he doeth?" They answered and said unto him, "Art thou also of Galilee? Search, and look: for out of Galilee ariseth no prophet." And every man went unto his own house.

THE WOMAN TAKEN IN ADULTERY

Jesus went unto the mount of Olives. And early in the morning he came again into the temple, and all the people came unto him; and he sat down, and taught them. And the scribes and Pharisees brought unto him a woman taken in adultery: and when they had set her in the midst, they say unto him, "Master, this woman was taken in adultery, in the very act. Now Moses in the law commanded us, that such should be stoned: but what sayest thou?" This they said, tempting him, that they might have to accuse him. But Jesus stooped down, and with *his* finger wrote on the ground, *as though he heard them not.* So when they continued asking him, he lifted up himself, and said unto them, "He that is without sin among you, let him first cast a stone at her." And again he stooped down, and wrote on the ground. And they which heard *it*, being convicted by *their own* conscience, went out one by one, beginning at the eldest, *even* unto the last: and Jesus was left alone, and the woman standing in the midst. When Jesus had lifted up himself, and saw none but the woman, he said unto her, "Woman, where are those thine accusers? hath no man condemned thee?" She said, "No man, Lord." And Jesus said unto her, "Neither do I condemn thee: go, and sin no more."

JESUS AND THE PHARISEES

Then spake Jesus again unto them, saying, "I am the light of the world: he that followeth me shall not walk in darkness, but shall have the light of life." The Pharisees therefore said unto him, "Thou bearest record of thyself; thy record is not true." Jesus answered and said unto them, "Though I bear record of myself, *yet* my record is true: for I know whence I came, and whither I go; but ye cannot tell whence I come, and whither I go. Ye judge after the flesh; I judge no man. And yet if I judge, my judgment is true: for I am not alone, but I and the Father that sent me. It is also written in your law, that the testimony of two men is true. I am one that bear witness of myself, and the Father that sent me beareth witness of me." Then said they unto him, "Where is thy Father?" Jesus answered, "Ye neither know me, nor my Father: if ye had known me, ye should have known my Father also." These words spake Jesus in the treasury, as he taught in the temple: and no man laid hands on him; for his hour was not yet come. Then said Jesus again unto them, "I go my way, and ye shall seek me, and shall die in your sins: whither I go, ye cannot come." Then said the Jews, "Will he kill himself?" because he saith, "Whither I go, ye cannot come." And he said unto them, "Ye are from beneath; I am from above: ye are of this world; I am not of this world. I said therefore unto you, that ye shall die in your sins: for if ye believe not that I am *he*, ye shall die in your sins." Then said they unto him, "Who art thou?" And Jesus saith unto them, "Even *the same* that I said unto you from the beginning. I have many things to say and to judge of you: but he that sent me is true; and I speak to the world those things which I have heard of him." They understood not that he spake to them of the Father. Then said Jesus unto them, "When ye have lifted up the Son of man, then shall ye know that I am *he*, and *that* I do nothing of myself; but as my Father hath taught me, I speak these things. And he that sent me is with me: the Father hath not left me alone; for I do always those things that please him." As he spake these words, many believed on him.

THE TRUTH

Then said Jesus to those Jews which believed on him, "If ye continue in my word, *then* are ye my disciples indeed; and ye shall know the truth, and the truth shall make you free." They answered him, "We be Abraham's seed, and were never in bondage to any man: how sayest thou, 'Ye shall be made free'?" Jesus answered them, "Verily, verily, I say unto you, Whosoever committeth sin is the servant of sin. And the servant abideth not in the house for ever: *but* the Son abideth ever. If the Son therefore shall make you free, ye shall be free indeed. I know that ye are Abraham's seed; but ye seek to kill me, because my word hath no place in you. I speak that which I have seen with my Father: and ye do that which ye have seen with your father." They answered and said unto him, "Abraham is our father." Jesus saith unto them, "If ye were Abraham's children, ye would do the works of Abraham. But now ye seek to kill me, a man that hath told you the truth, which I have heard of God: this did not Abraham. Ye do the deeds of your father." Then said they to him, "We be not born of fornication; we have one Father, *even* God." Jesus said unto them, "If God were your Father, ye would love me: for I proceeded forth and came from God; neither came I of myself, but he sent me. Why do ye not understand my speech? *even* because ye cannot hear my word. Ye are of *your* father the devil, and the lusts of your father ye will do. He was a murderer from the beginning, and abode not in the truth, because there is no truth in him. When he speaketh a lie, he speaketh of his own: for he is a liar, and the father of it. And because I tell *you* the truth, ye believe me not. Which of you convinceth me of sin? And if I say the truth, why do ye not believe me? He that is of God heareth God's words: ye therefore hear *them* not, because ye are not of God." Then answered the Jews, and said unto him, "Say we not well that thou art a Samaritan, and hast a devil?" Jesus answered, "I have not a devil; but I honour my Father, and ye do dishonour me. And I seek not mine own glory: there is one that seeketh and judgeth.

Verily, verily, I say unto you, If a man keep my saying, he shall never see death." Then said the Jews unto him, "Now we know that thou hast a devil. Abraham is dead, and the prophets; and thou sayest, 'If a man keep my saying, he shall never taste of death.' Art thou greater than our father Abraham, which is dead? and the prophets are dead: whom makest thou thyself?" Jesus answered, "If I honour myself, my honour is nothing: it is my Father that honoureth me; of whom ye say, that he is your God: yet ye have not known him; but I know him: and if I should say, 'I know him not,' I shall be a liar like unto you: but I know him, and keep his saying. Your father Abraham rejoiced to see my day: and he saw *it*, and was glad." Then said the Jews unto him, "Thou art not yet fifty years old, and hast thou seen Abraham?" Jesus said unto them, "Verily, verily, I say unto you, Before Abraham was, I am." Then took they up stones to cast at him: but Jesus hid himself, and went out of the temple, going through the midst of them, and so passed by.

THE LIGHT OF THE WORLD

And as *Jesus* passed by, he saw a man which was blind from *his* birth. And his disciples asked him, saying, "Master, who did sin, this man, or his parents, that he was born blind?" Jesus answered, "Neither hath this man sinned, nor his parents: but that the works of God should be made manifest in him. I must work the works of him that sent me, while it is day; the night cometh, when no man can work. As long as I am in the world, I am the light of the world.* When he had thus spoken, he spat on the ground, and made clay of the spittle, and he anointed the eyes of the blind man with the clay, and said unto him, "Go, wash in the pool of Siloam, (which is by interpretation, 'Sent.') He went his way therefore, and washed, and came seeing.

*This and the previous statement (see p. 60) are from the same passage in John, which indicates that both should be included.

The neighbours therefore, and they which before had seen him that he was blind, said, "Is not this he that sat and begged?" Some said, "This is he": others *said*, "He is like him": *but* he said, "I am *he*." Therefore said they unto him, "How were thine eyes opened?" He answered and said, "A man that is called Jesus made clay, and anointed mine eyes, and said unto me, 'Go to the pool of Siloam, and wash'; and I went and washed, and I received sight." Then said they unto him, "Where is he?" He said, "I know not."

They brought to the Pharisees him that aforetime was blind. And it was the sabbath day when Jesus made the clay, and opened his eyes. Then again the Pharisees also asked him how he had received his sight. He said unto them, "He put clay upon mine eyes, and I washed, and do see." Therefore said some of the Pharisees, "This man is not of God, because he keepeth not the sabbath day." Others said, "How can a man that is a sinner do such miracles?" And there was a division among them. They say unto the blind man again, "What sayest thou of him, that he hath opened thine eyes?" He said, "He is a prophet." But the Jews did not believe concerning him, that he had been blind, and received his sight, until they called the parents of him that had received his sight. And they asked them, saying, "Is this your son, who ye say was born blind? how then doth he now see?" His parents answered them and said, "We know that this is our son, and that he was born blind: but by what means he now seeth, we know not; or who hath opened his eyes, we know not: he is of age; ask him: he shall speak for himself." These *words* spake his parents, because they feared the Jews: for the Jews had agreed already, that if any man did confess that he was Christ, he should be put out of the synagogue. Therefore said his parents, "He is of age; ask him." Then again called they the man that was blind, and said unto him, "Give God the praise: we know that this man is a sinner." He answered and said, "Whether he be a sinner *or no*, I know not: one thing I know, that, whereas I was blind, now I see." Then said they to him again, "What did he to thee? how opened he thine eyes?" He answered them, "I have told you already, and ye did not hear: wherefore would ye hear *it* again? will ye also be his disciples?" Then they reviled him, and said, "Thou art his disciple; but we are Moses' disciples. We know that God spake unto Moses: *as for this fellow*, we know not from whence he is." The man answered and said unto them, "Why herein is a marvellous thing, that ye know not from whence he is, and *yet* he hath opened mine eyes. Now we know that God heareth not sinners: but if any man be a worshipper of God, and doeth his will, him he heareth. Since the world began was it not heard that any man opened the eyes of one that was born blind. If this man were not of God, he could do nothing." They answered and said unto him, "Thou wast altogether born in sins, and dost thou teach us?" And they cast him out. Jesus heard that they had cast him out; and when he had found him, he said unto him, "Dost thou believe on the Son of God?" He answered and said, "Who is he, Lord, that I might believe on him?" And Jesus said unto him, "Thou hast both seen him, and it is he that talketh with thee." And he said, "Lord, I believe." And he worshipped him.

And Jesus said, "For judgment I am come into this world, that they which see not might see; and that they which see might be made blind." And *some* of the Pharisees which were with him heard these words, and said unto him, "Are we blind also?" Jesus said unto them, "If ye were blind, ye should have no sin: but now ye say, 'We see'; therefore your sin remaineth.

PARABLE OF THE SHEEP

"Verily, verily, I say unto you, He that entereth not by the door into the sheepfold, but climbeth up some other way, the same is a thief and a robber. But he that entereth in by the door is the shepherd of the sheep. To him the porter openeth; and the sheep hear his voice: and he calleth his own sheep by name, and leadeth them out. And when he putteth forth his own sheep, he goeth before them, and the sheep follow him: for they know his voice. And a stranger will they not follow, but will flee from him: for they know not the voice of strangers." This parable spake Jesus unto them: but they understood not what things they were which he spake unto them. Then said Jesus unto them again, "Verily, verily, I say unto you, I am the door of the sheep. All that ever came before me are thieves and robbers: but the sheep did not hear them. I am the door: by me if any man enter in, he shall be saved, and shall go in and out, and find pasture. The thief cometh not, but for to steal, and to kill, and to destroy: I am come that they might have life, and that they might have *it* more abundantly. I am the good shepherd: the good shepherd giveth his life for the sheep. But he that is an hireling, and not the shepherd, whose own the sheep are not, seeth the wolf coming, and leaveth the sheep, and fleeth: and the wolf catcheth them, and scattereth the sheep. The hireling fleeth, because he is an hireling, and careth not for the sheep. I am the good shepherd, and know my *sheep*, and am known of mine. As the Father knoweth me, even so know I the Father: and I lay down my life for the sheep. And other sheep I have, which are not of this fold: them also I must bring, and they shall hear my voice; and there shall be one fold, *and* one shepherd. Therefore doth my Father love me, because I lay down my life, that I might take it again. No man taketh it from me, but I lay it down of myself. I have power to lay it down, and I have power to take it again. This commandment have I received of my Father."

"I AND MY FATHER ARE ONE"

There was a division therefore again among the Jews for these sayings. And many of them said, "He hath a devil, and is mad; why hear ye him?" Others said, "These are not the words of him that hath a devil. Can a devil open the eyes of the blind?"

And it was at Jerusalem the feast of the dedication, and it was

winter. And Jesus walked in the temple in Solomon's porch. Then
came the Jews round about him, and said unto him, "How long
dost thou make us to doubt? If thou be the Christ, tell us plainly."
Jesus answered them, "I told you, and ye believed not: the works
that I do in my Father's name, they bear witness of me. But ye
believe not, because ye are not of my sheep, as I said unto you. My
sheep hear my voice, and I know them, and they follow me: and I
give unto them eternal life; and they shall never perish, neither
shall any *man* pluck them out of my hand. My Father, which gave
them to me, is greater than all; and no *man* is able to pluck *them*
out of my Father's hand. I and *my* Father are one." Then the Jews
took up stones again to stone him. Jesus answered them, "Many
good works have I shewed you from my Father; for which of those
works do ye stone me?" The Jews answered him, saying, "For a
good work we stone thee not; but for blasphemy; and because
that thou, being a man, makest thyself God." Jesus answered
them, "Is it not written in your law, 'I said, Ye are gods'? If he
called them gods, unto whom the word of God came, and the
scripture cannot be broken; say ye of him, whom the Father hath
sanctified, and sent into the world, 'Thou blasphemest'; because I
said, I am the Son of God? If I do not the works of my Father,
believe me not. But if I do, though ye believe not me, believe the
works: that ye may know, and believe, that the Father *is* in me,
and I in him." Therefore they sought again to take him: but he
escaped out of their hand, and went away again beyond Jordan
into the place where John at first baptized; and there he abode.
And many resorted unto him, and said, "John did no miracle: but
all things that John spake of this man were true." And many
believed on him there.

MARTHA AND MARY

Now it came to pass, as they went, that he entered into a certain
village: and a certain woman named Martha received him into

her house.* And she had a sister called Mary, which also sat at Jesus' feet, and heard his word. But Martha was cumbered about much serving, and came to him, and said, "Lord, dost thou not care that my sister hath left me to serve alone? bid her therefore that she help me." And Jesus answered and said unto her, "Martha, Martha, thou art careful and troubled about many things: but one thing is needful: and Mary hath chosen that good part, which shall not be taken away from her."

JESUS AND HIS FAMILY

And it came to pass afterward, that he went throughout every city and village, preaching and shewing the glad tidings of the kingdom of God: and the twelve *were* with him. And certain women, which had been healed of evil spirits and infirmities, Mary called Magdalene, out of whom went seven devils, and Joanna the wife of Chuza Herod's steward, and Susanna, and many others, which ministered unto him of their substance.

Then came to him his mother and his brethren, while he yet talked to the people, desiring to speak with him, and, standing without, sent unto him, *as they* could not come at him for the press. And the multitude sat about him, and they said unto him, "Behold thy mother and thy brethren stand without, desiring to speak with thee." But he answered and said unto them, "Who is my mother? and who are my brethren?" And he looked around about on them and stretched forth his hand toward his disciples, and said, "Behold my mother and my brethren! For whosoever shall hear the word of God and do the will of my Father which is in heaven, the same is my brother, and sister, and mother."

*Luke did not seem to know Jesus' relationship with this family in Bethany. John felt that Jesus visited them right after the feast of dedication, although he places the raising of Lazarus at that point. This visit was at some point when he was near Jerusalem.

PARABLES OF THE SOWER

The same day went Jesus out of the house, and sat by the sea side. And great multitudes were gathered together unto him out of every city, so that he entered into a ship, and sat in the sea, and the whole multitude stood on the shore. And he taught them many things by parables, and said unto them in his doctrine, "Hearken; Behold a sower went forth to sow his seed: and it came to pass as he sowed, some fell by the way side, and it was trodden down, and the fowls of the air came and devoured it up. And some fell on stony ground, where it had not much earth; and immediately it sprang up because it had no depth of earth: but when the sun was up, it was scorched; and because it had no root, it withered away, because it lacked moisture. And some fell among thorns, and the thorns sprung up, and choked it, and it yielded no fruit. But other fell on good ground, and sprang up, and did yield fruit and increased; and brought forth fruit, some an hundredfold, some sixtyfold, some thirtyfold." And when he had said these things, he cried, "He that hath ears to hear, let him hear."

EXPLANATION OF THE PARABLE

And when he was alone, they that were about him with the twelve disciples came, and asked him what this parable might be, and said unto him, "why speakest thou unto them in parables?" And he answered and said unto them, "Because it is given unto you to know the mysteries of the kingdom of God [heaven—Matthew]: but to them that are without it is not given, all *these* things are done in parables. Therefore speak I to them in parables: that seeing they may see, and not perceive; and hearing they may hear, and not understand; lest at any time they should be converted, and *their* sins should be forgiven them. And in them is fulfilled the prophecy of Esaias, which saith, 'By hearing ye shall hear, and shall not understand; and seeing ye shall see, and shall not perceive: for this people's heart is waxed gross, and *their* ears are dull of hearing, and their eyes they have closed; lest at any time they should see with *their* eyes, and hear with *their* ears, and should understand with *their* heart, and should be converted, and I should heal them.' But blessed *are* your eyes, for they see: and your ears, for they hear. For verily I say unto you, that many prophets and righteous *men* have desired to see *those things* which ye see, and have not seen *them*; and to hear *those things* which ye hear, and have not heard them."

And he said unto them, "Know ye not this parable? and how then will ye know all parables? Hear ye then the parable of the sower. The seed is the word of God. The sower soweth the word. Those by the *way* side, where the word is sown are those that hear the word of the kingdom, and understand it not; but when they have heard the devil [Satan—Mark] cometh immediately, and taketh away the word that was sown in their hearts, lest they should believe and be saved. And they likewise that received the seed sown on stony ground, *are* they who, when they have heard the word, immediately receive it with joy; yet have no root in themselves, and so endure but for a time and for a while believe: afterward, when tribulation or affliction or persecution ariseth for the word's sake, immediately they are offended, and in a time of temptation fall away. And they that received the seed among the thorns are they which, when they have heard the word, go forth, and the cares of this world, the deceitfulness of riches, and the pleasures of *this* life, and the lusts of other things entering in, choke the word, and it becometh unfruitful [bring no fruit to perfection—Luke]. But those which are sown on good ground are they, which in an honest and good heart, hear the word, receive it, keep it, understand it, and bring forth fruit with patience, some an hundredfold, some sixty, some thirty. No man when he hath lighted a candle, covereth it with a vessel, or putteth it under a bed; but setteth *it* on a candlestick, that they which enter in may see the light.* For there is nothing hid, which shall not be manifested; neither was anything kept secret, that shall not be known and come abroad. If any man have ears to hear, let him hear." And he said unto them, "Take heed what ye hear: and unto you that hear shall more be given."

PARABLES OF THE KINGDOM OF GOD

And he said, "So is the kingdom of God, as if a man should cast seed into the ground; and should sleep, and rise night and day, and the seed should spring and grow up, he knoweth not how. For the earth bringeth forth fruit of herself; first the blade, then the ear, after that the full corn in the ear. But when the fruit is brought forth, immediately he putteth in the sickle, because the harvest is come.

"Whereunto shall we liken the kingdom of God? or with what comparison shall we compare it? The kingdom of heaven is likened unto a man which sowed good seed in his field: but while men slept, his enemy came and sowed tares among the wheat, and went his way. But when the blade was sprung up, and brought forth fruit, then appeared the tares also. So the servants of the householder came and said unto him, 'Sir, didst not thou sow good seed in thy field? from whence then hath it tares?' He said unto them, 'An enemy hath done this.' The servants said unto him, 'Wilt thou then that we go and gather them up?' But he said, 'Nay; lest while ye gather up the tares, ye root up also the wheat with them. Let both grow together until the harvest: and in the time of harvest I will say to the reapers, "Gather ye together first the tares, and bind them in bundles to burn them: but gather the wheat into my barn." ' "

*For the more familiar entry, see p. 38, in the Sermon on the Mount.

Another parable put he forth unto them, saying, "The kingdom of heaven is like to a grain of mustard seed, which a man took and sowed in his field; which indeed is the least of all seeds that be in the earth: but when it is grown, it is the greatest among herbs, and becometh a tree and shooteth out great branches, so that the birds of the air come and lodge in the branches thereof." Another parable spake he unto them: "The kingdom of heaven is like unto leaven, which a woman took, and hid in three measures of meal, till the whole was leavened."

All these things spake Jesus unto the multitude in parables as they were able to hear it; and without a parable spake he not unto them: that it might be fulfilled which was spoken by the prophet, saying, "I will open my mouth in parables; I will utter things which have been kept secret from the foundation of the world." Then Jesus sent the multitude away, and went into the house: and his disciples came unto him, saying, "Declare unto us the parable of the tares of the field." He answered and said unto them, "He that soweth the good seed is the Son of man; the field is the world; the good seed are the children of the kingdom; but the tares are the children of the wicked *one*; the enemy that sowed them is the devil; the harvest is the end of the world; and the reapers are the angels. As therefore the tares are gathered and burned in the fire; so shall it be in the end of this world. The Son of man shall send forth his angels, and they shall gather out of his kingdom all things that offend, and them which do iniquity; and shall cast them into a furnace of fire: there shall be wailing and gnashing of teeth. Then shall the righteous shine forth as the sun in the kingdom of their Father. Who hath ears to hear, let him hear.

"Again the kingdom of heaven is like unto treasure hid in a field; the which when a man hath found, he hideth, and for joy thereof goeth and selleth all that he hath, and buyeth that field. Again, the kingdom of heaven is like unto a merchant man, seeking goodly pearls: who, when he had found one pearl of great price, went and sold all that he had, and bought it. Again, the kingdom of heaven is like unto a net, that was cast into the sea, and gathered of every kind: which, when it was full, they drew to shore, and sat down, and gathered the good into vessels, but cast the bad away. So shall it be at the end of the world: the angels shall come forth, and sever the wicked from among the just, and shall cast them into the furnace of fire: there shall be wailing and gnashing of teeth." Jesus saith unto them, "Have ye understood all these things?" They say unto him, "Yea, Lord." Then said he unto them, "Therefore every scribe *which* is instructed unto the kingdom of heaven is like unto a man *that is* an householder, which bringeth forth out of his treasure *things* new and old."

Now when Jesus saw great multitudes about him, he gave commandment to depart unto the other side. And a certain scribe came, and said unto him, "Master, I will follow thee whithersoever thou goest." And Jesus saith unto him, "The foxes have holes, and the birds of the air *have* nests; but the Son of man hath not where to lay *his* head." And he said unto another of his disciples, "Follow me." But he said, "Lord, suffer me first to go and bury my father." But Jesus said unto him, "Follow me; and let the dead bury their dead: but go thou and preach the kingdom of God." And another also said, "Lord, I will follow thee; but let me first go bid them farewell, which are at home at my house." And Jesus said unto him, "No man, having put his hand to the plough, and looking back, is fit for the kingdom of God."

JESUS STILLS THE WAVES

And the same day when the even was come, he went into a ship, and his disciples followed him: and he said unto them, "Let us go over unto the other side of the lake." And when they had sent away the multitude, they took him even as he was in the ship. And there were also with him other little ships. And they launched forth. But as they sailed he fell asleep: and there arose a great storm of wind on the lake, and the waves beat into the ship insomuch that the ship was full of water, and they were in jeopardy. And he was in the hinder part of the ship, asleep on a pillow: and his disciples came to him, and awoke him, saying, "Master, master [Lord—Matthew], save us, carest thou not that we perish?" And he arose, and rebuked the wind and the raging of the water, and said to the sea, "Peace, be still." And the wind ceased, and there was a great calm. And he said unto them, "Why are ye so fearful, O ye of little faith? how is it that ye have no faith?" And they being exceedingly afraid wondered, saying one to another, "What manner of man is this, for he commandeth and even the wind and the sea obey him!"

JESUS CASTS OUT "LEGION"

And they came over unto the other side of the sea, into the country of the Gadarenes [Gergesenes—Matthew], which is over against Galilee. And when he was come out of the ship, immediately there met him a certain man [two men—Matthew] coming out of the tombs which had devils long time, and ware no clothes, neither abode in *any* house, but had *his* dwelling among the tombs; exceeding fierce, so that no man might pass by that way; and no man could bind him, no, not with chains: because that he had been often bound with fetters and chains, and the chains had been plucked asunder by him, and the fetters broken in pieces: neither could any *man* tame him. And always, night and day, he was in the mountains, and in the tombs, crying, and cutting himself with stones. But when he saw Jesus afar off, he ran and fell down before him and worshipped him, and cried out with a loud voice, saying, "What have I [we—Matthew] to do with thee, Jesus, thou Son of the most high God? art thou come hither to torment us before the time? I adjure [beseech—Luke] thee by God, that thou torment me not." (For he had commanded the unclean spirit, "Come out of the man, *thou* unclean spirit." For oftentimes it had caught him: and he was driven of the devil into the wilderness.) And Jesus asked him, saying, "What is thy name?" And he answered, "My name *is* Legion"; for many devils were entered into him. And they besought him that he would not command them to go out into the deep *or* send them away out of the country. And there was there an herd of many swine feeding on the mountain a good way off. And all the devils besought him, saying, "If thou cast us out, suffer us to go away into the herd of swine." And he suffered them. And he said unto them, "Go." Then the unclean spirits went out of the man, and entered into the swine: and, behold, the whole herd of swine ran violently down a steep place into the sea (they were about two thousand;) and were choked and perished in the sea. When they that fed the swine saw what was done, they fled, and went their ways into the city and told every thing, and what was befallen to the possessed of the devils in the city, and in the country. And, behold, the whole city went to see what it was that was done; and came to meet Jesus: and found the man that was possessed with the devil, and had the Legion out of whom the devils were departed, sitting at the feet of Jesus, and clothed, and in his right mind: and they were afraid. And they also that saw *it* told them how it befell to him that was possessed with the devil, by what means he was healed, and *also* concerning the swine. Then the whole multitude of the country of the Gadarenes round about besought him to depart from them and out of their coasts; for they were taken with great fear: and he went up into the ship.

Now the man that had been possessed with the devil, out of whom the devils were departed besought him that he might be with him: but Jesus suffered him not, but sent him away, saying, "Return to thine own house, to thy friends, and tell them how great things the Lord [God—Luke] hath done for thee, and hath had compassion on thee." And he went his way, and began to publish throughout the whole city of Decapolis how great things Jesus had done for him: and all *men* did marvel.

HEALING OF JAIRUS'S DAUGHTER

And it came to pass, when Jesus was returned again by ship unto the other side, they came into the land Gennesaret, and drew to the shore. And when they were come out of the ship, straightway much people gathered unto him and *gladly* received him: for they were all waiting for him, and they knew him and ran through that whole region round about, and began to carry about in beds those that were sick, where they heard he was. And whithersoever he entered, into villages, or cities, or country, they laid the sick in the streets, and besought him that they might touch if it were but the border of his garment: and as many as touched him were made whole.

And, behold, there cometh one of the rulers of the synagogue, Jairus by name: and when he saw him, he fell at his feet, and worshipped him, and besought him that he would come unto his house: for he had one only daughter, about twelve years of age, and she lay a dying, saying, "My little daughter lieth at the point of death [is even now dead—Matthew]: but come and lay thy hands on her, that she may be healed; and she shall live." And Jesus arose, and went with him, and *so did* his disciples. But as he went the people followed him and thronged him.

INTERLUDE: THE WOMAN WITH AN ISSUE OF BLOOD

And a certain woman, which had an issue of blood twelve years, and had suffered many things of many physicians, and had spent all she had upon physicians, neither could be healed of any, but rather grew worse, when she had heard of Jesus, came in the press behind *him*, and touched the hem of his garment. For she said within herself, "If I may touch but his garment, I shall be whole." And immediately the issue [fountain—Mark] of her blood was dried up; and she felt in *her* body that she was

healed of that plague. And Jesus, immediately knowing in himself that virtue had gone out of him, turned him about in the
press, and said, "Who touched me [my clothes—Mark]?" When
all denied, Peter and they that were with him said, "Master,
thou seest the multitude throng thee and press *thee*, and sayest
thou, 'Who touched me?'" And Jesus said, "Somebody hath
touched me: for I perceive that virtue is gone out of me." And he
looked round about to see her that had done this thing. And
when the woman saw that she was not hid, she came fearing
and trembling, knowing what was done in her, and falling
down before him, told him all the truth; she declared unto him
before all the people for what cause she had touched him, and
how she was healed immediately. And he said unto her,
"Daughter, be of good comfort: thy faith hath made thee whole;
go in peace, and be whole of thy plague." And the woman was
made whole from that hour.

While he yet spake, there cometh one from the ruler of the
synagogue's *house*, saying to him, "Thy daughter is dead: why
troublest thou the Master any further?" As soon as Jesus heard
the word that was spoken, he saith unto the ruler of the synagogue, "Fear not: only believe, and she shall be made whole."
And when he came into the house, he suffered no man to follow
him in, save Peter, and James, and John the brother of James,
and the father and the mother of the maiden. And when Jesus
came into the house of the ruler of the synagogue, he saw the
tumult, the minstrels and the people making noise, and them
that wept and wailed greatly. He said unto them, "Give place.
Why make ye this ado, and weep? the maid is not dead, but
sleepeth." And they laughed him to scorn, knowing that she was
dead. But when he had put them all out, he taketh the father
and the mother of the damsel, and them that were with him,
and entereth in where the damsel was lying. And he took the
damsel by the hand, and said unto her, "Talitha cumi"; which
is, being interpreted, "Damsel, I say unto thee, arise." And her
spirit came again, and she arose straightway, and walked; and

he commanded to give her meat. And her parents were astonished with a great astonishment: but he charged them straitly
that they should tell no man what was done. And the fame
hereof went abroad into all the land.

HEALS TWO BLIND MEN

And when Jesus departed thence, two blind men followed him,
crying and saying, "*Thou* son of David, have mercy on us." And
when he was come into the house, the blind men came to him:
and Jesus saith unto them, "Believe ye that I am able to do this?"
They said unto him, "Yea, Lord." Then touched he their eyes,
saying, "According to your faith be it unto you." And their eyes
were opened; and Jesus straitly charged them, saying, "See *that*
no man know *it.*" But they, when they were departed, spread
abroad his fame in all that country.

And Jesus went about all the cities and villages, teaching in
their synagogues, and preaching the gospel of the kingdom, and
healing every sickness and every disease among the people. But
when he saw the multitudes, he was moved with compassion
toward them, because they fainted, and were scattered abroad,
as sheep having no shepherd, and he began to teach them many
things. Then saith he unto his disciples, "The harvest truly *is*
plenteous, but the labourers *are* few; pray ye therefore the Lord of
the harvest, that he will send forth labourers into his harvest."

SENDING FORTH THE DISCIPLES

And he went out from thence, and came into his own country;
and his disciples follow him. And when the sabbath day was
come, he began to teach in the synagogue: and many hearing

him were astonished, saying, "From whence hath this *man* these things? and what wisdom *is* this which is given unto him, that even such mighty works are wrought by his hands? Is not this the carpenter, the carpenter's son, the son of Mary, the brother of James, and Joses, and of Juda, and Simon? and are not his sisters here with us? Whence then hath this *man* all these things?" And they were offended at him. But Jesus said unto them, "A prophet is not without honour, save in his own country, and among his own kin, and in his own house.* And he could there do no mighty work because of their unbelief, save that he laid his hands upon a few sick folk, and healed *them*. And he marvelled because of their unbelief. And he went round about the villages, teaching.

Then he called his twelve disciples together, and began to send them forth by two and two; and gave them power and authority over all unclean spirits [devils—Luke], and to cure diseases. And he sent them to preach the kingdom of God, and to heal the sick. And he said unto them, "Go not into the way of the Gentiles, and into *any* city of the Samaritans enter ye not: but go rather to the lost sheep of the house of Israel. And as ye go, preach, saying, 'The kingdom of heaven [God—Luke] is at hand.' Heal the sick, cleanse the lepers, raise the dead, cast out devils: freely ye have received, freely give. Provide neither gold, nor silver, nor brass in your purses, no bread, nor scrip for your journey, neither two coats, neither shoes, nor yet staves [save a staff only—Mark], but *be* shod with sandals: for the workman is worthy of his meat. And into whatsoever city or town ye shall enter, enquire who in it is worthy; and there abide till ye go thence. And when ye come into an house, salute it. And if the house be worthy, let your peace come upon it: but if it be not worthy, let your peace return to you. And whosoever shall not receive you, nor hear your words, when ye depart out of that house or city, shake off the dust of your feet for a testimony against them. Verily I say unto you, It shall be more tolerable for

---

*He seems to have said basically the same thing on a previous visit (see p. 29).

the land of Sodom and Gomorrha in the day of judgment, than for that city.* Behold, I send you forth as sheep in the midst of wolves: be ye therefore wise as serpents, and harmless as doves. But beware of men: for they will deliver you up to the councils, and they will scourge you in their synagogues; and ye shall be brought before governors and kings for my sake, for a testimony against them and the Gentiles. But when they deliver you up, take no thought how or what thing ye shall answer, or what ye shall say: for the Holy Ghost shall teach you in that same hour what ye ought to say. For it is not ye that speak, but the Spirit of your Father which speaketh in you.

"And the brother shall deliver up the brother to death, and the father the child: and the children shall rise up against *their* parents, and cause them to be put to death. And ye shall be hated of all *men* for my name's sake: but he that endureth to the end shall be saved. But when they persecute you in this city, flee ye into another: for verily I say unto you, Ye shall not have gone over the cities of Israel, till the Son of man be come. The disciple is not above *his* master, nor the servant above his lord. It is enough for the disciple that he be as his master, and the servant as his lord. If they have called the master of the house Beelzebub, how much more *shall they call* them of his household? Fear them not therefore: for there is nothing covered, that shall not be revealed: neither hid, that shall not be known. What I tell you in darkness, *that* speak ye in light: and what ye hear in the ear in closets, *that* preach [proclaim—Luke] ye upon the housetops.

"And I say unto you my friends, fear not them which kill the body, and after that have no more that they can do, but are not able to kill the soul: but I will forewarn you whom ye shall fear: fear him which after he has killed is able to destroy both soul and body in hell. Yea, I say unto you, Fear him. Are not two [five—Luke] sparrows sold for a farthing [two—Luke]? and one of them shall not fall on the ground without your Father [is not

*See p. 51 for a similar warning in a different context.

forgotten before God—Luke]. But the very hairs of your head are all numbered. Fear ye not therefore, ye are of more value than many sparrows. Whosoever therefore shall confess me before men, him will I [the Son of man—Luke] confess also before my Father [the angels of God—Luke] which is in heaven. But whosoever shall deny me before men, him will I also deny before my Father which is in heaven. Think not that I am come to send peace on earth: I came not to send peace, but a sword [rather division—Luke]. For I am come to set at variance the father against the son, and the son against the father; the mother against the daughter, and the daughter against the mother; the mother in law against her daughter in law, and the daughter in law against her mother in law. And a man's foes *shall be* they of his own household. For from henceforth there shall be five in one house divided, three against two and two against three. He that loveth father or mother more than me is not worthy of me: and he that loveth son or daughter more than me is not worthy of me. And he that taketh not his cross, and followeth after me, is not worthy of me. He that findeth his life shall lose it: and he that loseth his life for my sake shall find it.

"Verily, verily, I say unto you, he that receiveth whomsoever I send [you—Matthew] receiveth me, and he that receiveth me receiveth him that sent me. He that receiveth a prophet in the name of a prophet shall receive a prophet's reward; and he that receiveth a righteous man in the name of a righteous man shall receive a righteous man's reward. And whosoever shall give to drink unto one of these little ones a cup of cold *water* only in the name of a disciple, verily I say unto you, he shall in no wise lose his reward." And it came to pass, when Jesus had made an end of commanding his twelve disciples, they went out, and went through the towns, preaching the gospel, that men should repent. And they cast out many devils, and anointed with oil many that were sick, and healed *them* everywhere. And he departed thence to teach and to preach in their cities.

DEATH OF JOHN THE BAPTIST

Now Herod the tetrarch heard of all that was done by him (for his name was spread abroad:) and he was perplexed and said unto his servants [it was said of some—Luke], "This is John the Baptist; he is risen from the dead, and therefore mighty works do shew forth themselves in him." Others said, "That it is Elias that had appeared." And others said, "That it is a prophet, or one of the old prophets was risen again." But when Herod heard *thereof*, he said, "John I have beheaded: but who is this, of whom I hear such things?" And he desired to see him. For Herod himself had sent forth and laid hold upon John, and bound him and put him in prison for Herodias' sake, his brother Philip's wife: for he had married her. For John had said unto Herod, "It is not lawful for thee to have thy brother's wife." Therefore Herodias had a quarrel against him, and would have killed him; but she could not: for Herod feared John, knowing that he was a just man and an holy, and observed him; and when he heard him, he did many things, and heard him gladly. And when he would have put him to death, he feared the multitude, because they counted him as a prophet.

And when a convenient day was come, that Herod on his birthday made a supper to his lords, high captains, and chief *estates* of Galilee; and when the daughter of the said Herodias came in, and danced, and pleased Herod and them that sat with him, the king said unto the damsel, "Ask of me whatsoever thou wilt, and I will give *it* thee." And he sware unto her, "Whatsoever thou shalt ask of me, I will give *it* thee, unto the half of my kingdom." And she went forth, and said unto her mother, "What shall I ask?" And she said, "The head of John the Baptist." And she came in straightway with haste unto the king, and asked, saying, "I will that thou give me by and by in a charger the head of John the Baptist." And the king was exceeding sorry; *yet* for his oath's sake, and for their sakes which sat with him, he would not reject her. And immediately the king sent an executioner, and commanded his head to be brought: and he went and beheaded him in the prison, and brought his head in a charger, and gave it to the damsel: and the damsel gave it to her mother. And when his disciples heard *of it*, they came and took up his corpse, and laid it in a tomb and went and told Jesus.

RETURN OF THE DISCIPLES

And the apostles, when they were returned, gathered themselves together unto Jesus, and told him all things, both what they had done, and what they had taught.

FEEDING OF THE FIVE THOUSAND

And he said unto them, "Come ye yourselves apart into a desert place, and rest a while": for there were many coming and going, and they had no leisure so much as to eat. And they departed thence privately by ship over the sea of Galilee, which is *the sea* of Tiberias, into a desert place belonging to the city called Bethsaida. And the people saw them departing, and many knew him, and ran on foot thither out of all cities, and outwent them,* and came together unto him, because they saw his miracles which he did on them that were diseased. And Jesus went up into a mountain, and there sat with his disciples, and he received them, and he began to teach them many things, and spake unto them of the kingdom of God, and healed their sick that had need of healing. And the passover, a feast of the Jews, was nigh. And when the day was now far spent, his twelve disciples came unto him, saying, "This is a desert place, and the time is now far passed. Send the multitude away, that they may

*The distances in this story are all within a space of five miles.

go into the country round about, and into the villages, and lodge, and buy themselves bread and victuals: for they have nothing to eat, for we are here in a desert place." When Jesus then lifted up *his* eyes, and saw the great multitude, he answered and said unto them, "They need not depart: give ye them to eat." He saith unto Philip, "Whence shall we buy bread, that these may eat?" And this he said to prove him: for he himself knew what he would do. Philip answered him, "Two hundred pennyworth of bread is not sufficient for them, that every one of them may take a little. Shall we go and buy and give them to eat?" He saith unto them, "How many loaves have ye? go and see." One of his disciples, Andrew, Simon Peter's brother, saith unto him, "There is a lad here, which hath five barley loaves, and two small fishes: what are they among so many, except we should go and buy meat for all these people." He said, "Bring them hither to me." And he commanded his disciples to make the multitude all sit down by companies upon the green grass. (Now there was much green grass in that place.) And they did so and made them all sit down. And they sat down in ranks, by hundreds, and by fifties in a company.

And when he had taken the five loaves and the two fishes, he looked up to heaven, and blessed, and brake the loaves, and when he had given thanks, he distributed the loaves to his disciples to set before the multitude that were set down; and the two fishes he divided among them all as much as they would. And they all did eat, and were filled. When they were filled, he said unto his disciples, "Gather up the fragments that remain, that nothing be lost." Therefore they gathered *them* together, and filled twelve baskets with the fragments of the five barley loaves and of the fishes, which remained over and above unto them that had eaten. And they that had eaten were about five thousand men, beside women and children. Then those men, when they had seen the miracle that Jesus did, said, "This is of a truth that prophet that should come into the world." When Jesus perceived that they would come and take him by force, to make him a king, he straightway constrained his disciples to get into a ship, and to go before him unto the other side unto Bethsaida, while he sent the multitudes away. And when he had sent the multitudes away, he went up into a mountain apart to pray alone.

WALKS ON WATER

And when even was *now* come, his disciples went down unto the sea, and entered into a ship, and went over the sea toward Capernaum. And when it was dark, the ship was in the midst of the sea, and he was there alone on the land, and was not come to them. And the sea arose by reason of a great wind that blew. And he saw them toiling in rowing, tossed with waves, for the wind was contrary unto them. And about the fourth watch of the night, when they had rowed about five and twenty or thirty furlongs, Jesus cometh unto them, walking upon the sea, and drawing nigh unto the ship, and would have passed by them. But when the disciples saw him walking upon the sea, they supposed it had been a spirit: and they were troubled, and cried out for fear. But immediately Jesus talked with them, saying, "Be of good cheer: it is I; be not afraid." And Peter answered him and said, "Lord, if it be thou, bid me come unto thee on the water." And he said, "Come." And when Peter was come down out of the ship, he walked on the water, to go to Jesus. But when he saw the wind boisterous, he was afraid: and beginning to sink, he cried, saying, "Lord, save me." And immediately Jesus stretched forth *his* hand, and caught him, and said unto him, "O thou of little faith, wherefore didst thou doubt?" Then they willingly received him into the ship: and when they were come into the ship, the wind ceased: and they were sore amazed in themselves beyond measure, and wondered. For they considered not *the miracle* of the loaves: for their heart was hardened. Then they that were in the ship came and worshipped him, saying, "Of a truth thou art the Son of God." And immediately the ship was at the land of Gennesaret whither they went.

THE BREAD OF LIFE

The day following, when the people which stood on the other side of the sea saw that there was none other boat there, save that one whereinto his disciples were entered, and that Jesus went not with his disciples into the boat, but *that* his disciples were gone away alone; (howbeit there came other boats from Tiberias nigh unto the place where they did eat bread, after that the Lord had given thanks:) when the people therefore saw that Jesus was not there, neither his disciples, they also took shipping, and came to Capernaum, seeking for Jesus. And when they had found him on the other side of the sea, they said unto him, "Rabbi, when camest thou hither?" Jesus answered them and said, "Verily, verily, I say unto you, Ye seek me, not because ye saw the miracles, but because ye did eat of the loaves, and were filled. Labour not for the meat which perisheth, but for that meat which endureth unto everlasting life, which the Son of man shall give unto you: for him hath God the Father sealed." Then said they unto him, "What shall we do that we might work the works of God?" Jesus answered and said unto them, "This is the work of God, that ye believe on him whom he hath sent." They said therefore unto him, "What sign shewest thou then, that we may see, and believe thee? what dost thou work? Our fathers did eat manna in the desert; as it is written, 'He gave them bread from heaven to eat.' " Then Jesus said unto them, "Verily, verily, I say unto you, Moses gave you not that bread from heaven; by my Father giveth you the true bread from heaven. For the bread of God is he which cometh down from heaven, and giveth life unto the world." Then said they unto him, "Lord, evermore give us this bread." And Jesus said unto them, "I am the bread of life: he that cometh to me shall never hunger; and he that believeth on me shall never thirst. But I said unto you, That ye also have seen me, and believe not. All that the Father giveth me shall come to me; and him that cometh to me I will in no wise cast out. For I came down from heaven, not to do mine own will, but the will of him that sent me. And this is the Father's will which hath sent me, that of all which he hath given me I should lose nothing, but should raise it up again at the last day. And this is the will of him that sent me, that every one which seeth the Son, and believeth on him, may have everlasting life: and I will raise him up at the last day." The Jews then murmured at him, because he said, "I am the bread which came down from heaven." And they said, "Is not this Jesus, the son of Joseph, whose father and mother we know? how is it then that he saith, "I came down from heaven?" " Jesus therefore answered and said unto them, "Murmur not among yourselves. No man can come to me except the Father which hath sent me draw him: and I will raise him up at the last day. It is written in the prophets, 'And they shall be all taught of God.' Every man therefore that hath heard, and hath learned of the Father, cometh unto me. Not that any man hath seen the Father, save he which is of God, he hath seen the Father. Verily, verily, I say unto you, He that believeth on me hath everlasting life. I am that bread of life. Your fathers did eat manna in the wilderness, and are dead. This is the bread which cometh down from heaven, that a man may eat thereof, and not die. I am the living bread which came down from heaven: if any man eat of this bread, he shall live for ever: and the bread that I will give is my flesh, which I will give for the life of the world." The Jews therefore strove among themselves, saying, "How can this man give us *his* flesh to eat?" Then Jesus said unto them, "Verily, verily, I say unto you, Except ye eat the flesh of the Son of man, and drink his blood, ye have no life in you. Whoso eateth my flesh, and drinketh my blood, hath eternal life; and I will raise him up at the last day. For my flesh is meat indeed, and my blood is drink indeed. He that eateth my flesh, and drinketh my blood, dwelleth in me, and I in him. As the living Father hath sent me, and I live by the Father: so he that eateth me, even he shall live by me. This is that bread which came down from heaven: not as your fathers did eat manna, and are dead: he that eateth of this bread shall live for ever."

SOME DISCIPLES FALL AWAY

These things said he in the synagogue, as he taught in Capernaum. Many therefore of his disciples, when they had heard *this*, said, "This is an hard saying: who can hear it?" When Jesus knew in himself that his disciples murmured at it, he said unto them, "Doth this offend you? *What* and if ye shall see the Son of man ascend up where he was before? It is the spirit that quickeneth: the flesh profiteth nothing: the words that I speak unto you, *they* are spirit, and *they* are life. But there are some of you that believe not." For Jesus knew from the beginning who they were that believed not, and who should betray him. And he said, "Therefore said I unto you, that no man can come unto me, except it were given unto him of my Father." From that *time* many of his disciples went back, and walked no more with him. Then said Jesus unto the twelve, "Will ye also go away?" Then Simon Peter answered him, "Lord, to whom shall we go? thou hast the words of eternal life." Jesus answered them, "Have not I chosen you twelve, and one of you is a devil?" He spake of Judas Iscariot *the son* of Simon: for he it was that should betray him, being one of the twelve.

JESUS AND THE PHARISEES

Then came together unto him the Pharisees, and certain of the scribes, which came from Jerusalem. And when they saw some of his disciples eat bread with defiled, that is to say, with unwashen, hands, they found fault. For the Pharisees, and all the Jews, except they wash *their* hands oft, eat not, holding the tradition of the elders. And *when they come* from the market, except they wash, they eat not. And many other things there be, which they have received to hold, *as* the washing of cups, and pots, brasen vessels, and of tables. Then the Pharisees and scribes asked him, "Why walk not thy disciples according to the tradition of the elders, for they wash not their hands, when they eat bread?" He answered and said unto them, "Well hath Esaias prophesied of you hypocrites, as it is written, 'This people draweth nigh unto me with their mouth, and honoureth me with *their* lips, but their heart is far from me. Howbeit in vain do they worship me, teaching *for* doctrines the commandments of men.' Why do ye also transgress the commandment of God by your tradition? For laying aside the commandment of God, ye hold the tradition of men, *as* the washing of pots and cups: and many other such like things ye do." And he said unto them, "Full well ye reject the commandment of God, that ye may keep your own tradition. For Moses said, 'Honour thy father and thy mother'; and, 'Whoso curseth father or mother, let him die the death': but ye say, 'If a man shall say to his father or mother, "It is Corban, that is to say, a gift, by whatsoever thou mightest be profited by me"; and honour not his father and mother, *he shall be free.*' And ye suffer him no more to do ought for his father or his mother; making the word of God of none effect through your tradition, which ye have delivered: and many such like things do ye."

And when he had called all the people unto him, he said unto them, "Hearken unto me every one of you, and understand: there is nothing from without which entereth into the mouth that defileth a man; but that which cometh out of the mouth, this defileth a man. If any man have ears to hear, let him hear." Then came his disciples, and said unto him, "Knowest thou that the Pharisees were offended, after they heard this saying?" But he answered and said, "Every plant, which my heavenly Father hath not planted, shall be rooted up. Let them alone: they be blind leaders of the blind. And if the blind lead the blind, both shall fall into the ditch."*

And when he was entered in the house from the people, Peter said unto him, "Declare unto us this parable." And Jesus said,

*For a similar statement, see p. 43.

"Are ye also yet so without understanding? Do ye not yet understand that whatsoever thing from without entereth in at the mouth, goeth into the belly, and is cast out into the draught, purging all meats, *it* cannot defile him because it entereth not into his heart? But those things which proceed out of the mouth come forth from the heart; and they defile the man. For from within, out of the heart of men, proceed evil thoughts, adulteries, fornications, murders, thefts, covetousness, wickedness, deceit, lasciviousness, an evil eye, false witness, blasphemy, pride, foolishness: all these evil things come from within and defile the man: but to eat with unwashen hands defileth not a man."

JESUS GOES ON WIDER JOURNEYS

Then Jesus arose *and* went thence, and departed into the coasts of Tyre and Sidon, and entered into an house, and would have no man know it, but he could not be hid. For a *certain* woman, whose young daughter had an unclean spirit, heard of him, and came and fell at his feet: the woman was a Greek, a Syrophenician by nation [of Canaan—Matthew]; and she besought him that he would cast forth the devil out of her daughter, saying, "Have mercy on me, O Lord, *thou* son of David; for my daughter is grievously vexed with a devil." But he answered her not a word. And his disciples came and besought him, saying, "Send her away; for she crieth after us." But Jesus answered and said unto her, "I am not sent but unto the lost sheep of the house of Israel. Let the children first be filled: for it is not meet to take the children's bread, and to cast *it* unto the dogs." Then came she and worshipped him, saying, "Lord, help me. Truth, Lord: yet the dogs under the table eat of the children's crumbs which fall from their masters' table." Then Jesus answered and said unto her, "Woman, great *is* thy faith. For this saying go thy way: be it unto thee even as thou wilt; the devil is gone out of thy daughter." And her daughter was made whole from that very hour. And when she was come to her house, she found the devil gone out, and her daughter laid upon the bed.

HEALS A DEAF AND DUMB MAN

And again, departing from the coast of Tyre and Sidon, he came unto the sea of Galilee, through the midst of the coast of Decapolis, and went up into a mountain, and sat down there. And great multitudes came unto him, having with them *those that were* lame, blind, dumb, maimed, and many others, and cast them down at Jesus' feet; and he healed them: insomuch that the multitude wondered, when they saw the dumb to speak, the maimed to be whole, the lame to walk, and the blind to see: and they glorified the God of Israel. And they bring unto him one that was deaf, and had an impediment in his speech; and they beseech him to put his hand upon him. And he took him aside from the multitude, and put his fingers into his ears, and he spit, and touched his tongue; and looking up to heaven, he sighed, and saith unto him, "Ephpatha," that is, "Be opened." And straightway his ears were opened, and the string of his tongue was loosed, and he spake plain. And he charged them that they should tell no man: but the more he charged them, so much the more a great deal they published *it;* and were beyond measure astonished, saying, "He hath done all things well: he maketh both the deaf to hear, and the dumb to speak."

FEEDING OF THE FOUR THOUSAND

In those days the multitude being very great, and having nothing to eat, Jesus called his disciples *unto him,* and saith unto them, "I have compassion on the multitude, because thay have now been with me three days, and have nothing to eat: I will not send them away fasting, for if I send them away fasting to their own houses, they will faint by the way; for divers of them came from far.* And his disciples say unto him, "From whence should we have so much bread in the wilderness to satisfy so great a multitude?" And he asked them, "How many loaves have ye?" And they said, "Seven." And he commanded the people to sit down on the ground: and he took the seven loaves, and gave thanks, and brake, and gave to his disciples to set before *them;* and they did set *them* before the people. And they had a few small fishes: and he blessed, and commanded to set them also before *them.* So they did all eat, and were filled, and they took up the broken *meat* that was left seven baskets full. And they that had eaten were about four thousand: and he sent them away. And straightway he entered into a ship with his disciples, and came into the parts of Dalmanutha [Magdala—Matthew].

Now *the disciples* had forgotten to take bread, neither had they in the ship with them more than one loaf. And he charged them, saying, "Take heed, beware of the leaven of the Pharisees, and of the Sadducees, and *of* the leaven of Herod." And they reasoned among themselves, saying, "*It is* because we have taken no bread." And when Jesus knew *it,* he saith unto them, "Why reason ye, because ye have no bread? perceive ye not yet, neither understand? have ye your heart yet hardened? Having eyes, see ye not? and having ears, hear ye not? and do ye not remember? When I brake the five loaves among five thousand, how many baskets full of fragments took ye up?" They say unto him, "Twelve." "And when the seven among four thousand, how many baskets full of fragments took ye up?" And they said, "Seven." And he said unto them, "How is it that ye do not understand? that I spake *it* not to you concerning bread, that ye should beware of the leaven of the Pharisees and of the Saddu-

*Mark and Matthew make the point clear a little later that there were two miraculous feedings.

cees?" Then understood they how that he bade *them* not beware of the leaven of bread, but of the doctrine of the Pharisees and of the Sadducees.

HEALS A BLIND MAN

And he cometh to Bethsaida; and they bring a blind man unto him, and besought him to touch him. And he took the blind man by the hand, and led him out of town; and when he had spit on his eyes, and put his hands upon him, he asked him if he saw ought. And he looked up, and said, "I see men as trees, walking." After that he put *his* hands again upon his eyes, and made him look up: and he was restored, and saw every man clearly. And he sent him away to his house, saying, "Neither go into the town, nor tell *it* to any in the town."

PETER'S DECLARATION

And Jesus went out, and his disciples, into the towns of Caesarea Philippi. And it came to pass, as he was alone praying, and his disciples were with him, he asked his disciples, saying, "Whom do men say that I the Son of man am?" And they said, "Some *say that thou art* John the Baptist: some, Elias; and others, Jeremias, or one of the old prophets risen again." He saith unto them, "But whom say ye that I am?" And Simon Peter answered and said, "We believe and are sure that thou art the Christ, the Son of the living God." And Jesus answered and said unto him, "Blessed art thou, Simon Bar-Jona: for flesh and blood hath not revealed *it* unto thee, but my Father which is in heaven. And I say also unto thee, That thou art Peter, and upon this rock I will build my church; and the gates of hell shall not prevail against it. And I will give unto thee the keys of the kingdom of heaven:

and whatsoever thou shalt bind on earth shall be bound in heaven: and whatsoever thou shalt loose on earth shall be loosed in heaven." Then charged he his disciples that they should tell no man that he was Jesus the Christ.

And they departed thence, and passed through Galilee, and he would not that any man should know it [And they were in the way going up to Jerusalem; and Jesus went before them: and they were amazed; and as they followed, they were afraid— Mark]; and from that time forth while they abode in Galilee, Jesus took again the twelve apart in the way and began to shew unto his disciples what things should happen unto him, saying, "Behold, we go up to Jerusalem: and all things that are written by the prophets concerning the Son of man shall be accomplished. Let these sayings sink down into your ears: for the Son of man shall be delivered [betrayed—Matthew] into the hands of the chief priests, and unto the scribes and elders; and they shall condemn him to death, and shall deliver him to the Gentiles: and they shall mock him, and shall scourge him, and shall spit upon him, and shall kill [crucify—Matthew] him: and after that he is killed, he shall rise again the third day." And he spake these sayings openly. And they were exceeding sorry, but they understood none of these sayings, and it was hid from them, neither perceived they things which were spoken: and they were afraid to ask him of that saying.

Then Peter took him and began to rebuke him, saying, "Be it far from thee, Lord: this shall not be unto thee." But when he had turned about and looked on his disciples, he rebuked Peter, saying, "Get thee behind me, Satan: thou art an offence unto me: for thou savourest not the things that be of God, but the things that be of men."

And when he had called the people *unto him* with his disciples also, he said unto them, "Whosoever will come after me, let him deny himself, and take up his cross daily; and follow me. For whosoever will save his life shall lose it: but whosoever shall lose his life for my sake and the gospel's, the same shall save it. For what shall it profit a man, if he shall gain the whole world, and lose his own soul? Or what shall a man give in exchange for his soul? Whosoever therefore shall be ashamed of me and of my words in this adulterous and sinful generation; of him also shall the Son of man be ashamed, when he cometh in his own glory, and in the glory of his Father with the holy angels; and then he shall reward every man according to his works." And he said unto them, "Verily I say unto you, That there be some of them that stand here, which shall not taste of death, till they have seen the Son of man coming in the kingdom of God [his—Matthew] with power."

THE TRANSFIGURATION

And it came to pass after six [about eight—Luke] days after these sayings, Jesus taketh Peter, James, and John his brother, and leadeth them up into a high mountain apart by themselves to pray. And as he prayed, he was transfigured before them: the fashion of his countenance was altered, and his face did shine as the sun, and his raiment became shining [glistering—Luke], exceeding white as snow *or* as the light; so as no fuller on earth can white them. And, behold, there appeared unto them Moses and Elias, who appeared in glory; and they were talking with Jesus, and spake of his decease which he should accomplish at Jerusalem. But Peter and they that were with him were heavy with sleep: and when they were awake, they saw his glory, and the two men that stood with him. And it came to pass, as they departed from him, Peter answered and said unto Jesus, "Master [Lord—Matthew], it is good for us to be here: if thou wilt, let us make here three tabernacles; one for thee, and one for Moses, and one for Elias." For he wist not what to say; for they were sore afraid. While he thus spake, there came a bright cloud and overshadowed them: and they feared as they entered into the cloud. And behold there came a voice out of the cloud, which said, "This is my beloved Son, in whom I am well pleased; hear him." And when the disciples heard *it*, they fell on their face, and were sore afraid. And when the voice was past, suddenly, when they had looked round about, they saw no man any more, save Jesus alone with themselves. And Jesus came and touched them, and said, "Arise, and be not afraid." And as they came down from the mountain, Jesus charged them, saying, "Tell the vision to no man, until the Son of man be risen from the dead." And they kept it close, and told no man in those days any of those things which they had seen. And questioning one with another what the rising from the dead should mean, his disciples asked him, saying, "Why then say the scribes that Elias must first come?" And Jesus answered and said unto them, "Elias truly shall come first and restore all things. Likewise shall also the Son of man suffer many things, and be set at nought. But I say unto you, That Elias is indeed come already, and they knew him not, but have done unto him whatsoever they listed, as it is written of him." Then the disciples understood that he spake unto them of John the Baptist.

CURING THE EPILEPTIC BOY

And it came to pass, that on the next day, when they were come down from the hill, when he came to *his* disciples, he saw a great multitude about them, and the scribes questioning with them. And straightway all the people, when they beheld him, were greatly amazed, and running to *him*, saluted him. And he asked the scribes, "What question ye with them?" And, behold, a man of the company came to him, kneeling down to him, and cried out, saying, "Master [Lord—Matthew], I have brought unto thee my son, which hath a dumb spirit; I beseech thee, look upon my son *and* have mercy: for he is mine only child: for he is lunatick, and sore vexed: and wheresoever the spirit taketh him, he teareth him, and he suddenly crieth out: and he foameth, and gnasheth with his teeth, and pineth away; and *the* *spirit* bruising him hardly departeth from him. And I brought him to thy disciples: and I spake to *them* and besought *them* to cast him out; and they could not cure him." And Jesus answered him and said, "O faithless and perverse generation, how long shall I be with you? how long shall I suffer you? bring him hither to me." And they brought him unto him: and when he saw him, straightway the spirit tare him; and he fell on the ground, and wallowed foaming. And he asked his father, "How long is it ago since this came unto him?" And he said, "Of a child. And ofttimes it hath cast him into the fire, and into the waters, to destroy him: but if thou canst do any thing, have compassion on us, and help us." Jesus said unto him, "If thou canst believe, all things are possible to him that believeth." And straightway the father of the child cried out, and said with tears, "Lord, I believe; help thou mine unbelief." When Jesus saw that the people came running together, he rebuked the foul spirit, saying unto him, "Thou dumb and deaf spirit, I charge thee, come out of him, and enter no more into him." And *the spirit* cried, and rent him sore, and came out of him: and he was as one dead: insomuch that many said, "He is dead." But Jesus took him by the hand, and lifted him up and delivered him again to his father and he arose. And they were all amazed at the mighty power of God. And when he was come into the house, his disciples asked him privately, "Why could not we cast him out?" And Jesus said unto them, "Because of your unbelief: for verily I say unto you, If ye have faith as a grain of mustard seed, ye shall say unto this mountain, 'Remove hence to yonder place'; and it shall remove:* and nothing shall be impossible unto you. Howbeit this kind goeth not out but by prayer and fasting."

And when they were come to Capernaum, they that received tribute *money* came to Peter, and said, "Doth not your master pay tribute?" He saith, "Yes." And when he was come into the house, Jesus prevented him, saying, "What thinkest thou, Simon?

*See pp. 113 and 131.

of whom do the kings of the earth take custom or tribute? of their own children, or of strangers?" Peter saith unto him, "Of strangers." Jesus saith unto him, "Then are the children free. Notwithstanding, lest we should offend them, go thou to the sea, and cast an hook, and take up the fish that first cometh up; and when thou hast opened his mouth, thou shalt find a piece of money: that take, and give unto them for me and thee."

JESUS TEACHES TRUE DISCIPLESHIP

And being in a house in Capernaum he asked them, "What was it that ye disputed among yourselves by the way?" But they held their peace: for by the way they had disputed among themselves which of them should be accounted the greatest. *Then* the disciples came unto Jesus, saying, "Who is the greatest in the kingdom of heaven?" And Jesus, perceiving the thought of their heart, sat down, and called the twelve, and saith unto them, "If any man desire to be first, *the same* shall be last of all, and servant of all, for he that is least among you all, the same shall be great." And he called a little child unto him, and set him in the midst of them by him; and when he had taken him in his arms, he said unto them, "Verily I say unto you, Except ye be converted, and become as little children, ye shall not enter into the kingdom of heaven. Whosoever therefore shall humble himself as this little child, the same is greatest in the kingdom of heaven. Whosoever shall receive one such little child in my name receiveth me; but whosoever shall receive me, receiveth not me, but him that sent me. But whoso shall offend one of these little ones which believe in me, it were better for him that a millstone were hanged about his neck, and *that* he were drowned in the depth of the sea.

"Woe unto the world because of offences! for it must needs be that offences come; but woe to that man by whom the offence cometh! And if thy hand offend thee, cut it off: it is better for thee to enter into life maimed, than having two hands to go into hell, into the fire that never shall be quenched: where their worm dieth not, and the fire is not quenched.* And if thy foot offend thee, cut it off: it is better for thee to enter halt into life, than having two feet to be cast into hell, into the fire that never shall be quenched: where their worm dieth not, and the fire is not quenched. And if thine eye offend thee, pluck it out: it is better for thee to enter into the kingdom of God with one eye, than having two eyes to be cast into hell fire: where their worm dieth not, and the fire is not quenched. For every one shall be salted with fire, and every sacrifice shall be salted with salt, but if the salt have lost his saltness, wherewith will ye season it?[†] Have salt in yourselves, and have peace one with another.

"Take heed that ye despise not one of these little ones; for I say unto you, That in heaven their angels do always behold the face of my Father which is in heaven. For the Son of man is come to save that which was lost. How think ye? If a man have an hundred sheep, and one of them be gone astray, doth he not leave the ninety and nine, and goeth into the mountains, and seeketh that which is gone astray?[‡] And if so be that he find it, verily I say unto you, he rejoiceth more of that *sheep*, than of the ninety and nine which went not astray. Even so it is not the will of your Father which is in heaven, that one of these little ones should perish.

"Moreover if thy brother shall trespass against thee, go and tell him his fault between thee and him alone: if he shall hear thee, thou hast gained thy brother. But if he will not hear *thee*, *then* take with thee one or two more, that in the mouth of two or three witnesses every word may be established. And if he shall neglect to hear them, tell *it* unto the church: but if he neglect to hear the church, let him be unto thee as an heathen man and a publican. Verily I say unto you, whatsoever ye shall

---

*For a shorter form of this, see the Sermon on the Mount, p. 39.

†Also in the Sermon on the Mount, see p. 37.

‡He repeats this parable very soon, see pp. 109–110.

bind on earth shall be bound in heaven: and whatsoever ye shall loose on earth shall be loosed in heaven.* Again I say unto you, That if two of you shall agree on earth as touching any thing that they shall ask, it shall be done for them of my Father which is in heaven. For where two or three are gathered together in my name, there am I in the midst of them."

ON FORGIVENESS

Then came Peter to him, and said, "Lord, how oft shall my brother sin against me, and I forgive him? till seven times?" Jesus saith unto him, "I say not unto thee, Until seven times: but, Until seventy times seven. Therefore is the kingdom of heaven likened unto a certain king, which would take account of his servants. And when he had begun to reckon, one was brought unto him, which owed him ten thousand talents. But forasmuch as he had not to pay, his lord commanded him to be sold, and his wife, and children, and all that he had, and payment to be made. The servant therefore fell down, and worshipped him, saying, "Lord, have patience with me, and I will pay thee all." Then the lord of that servant was moved with compassion, and loosed him, and forgave him the debt. But the same servant went out, and found one of his fellowservants, which owed him an hundred pence: and he laid hands on him, and took *him* by the throat, saying, 'Pay me that thou owest.' And his fellowservant fell down at his feet, and besought him, saying, 'Have patience with me, and I will pay thee all.' And he would not: but went and cast him into prison, till he should pay the debt. So when his fellowservants saw what was done, they were very sorry, and came and told unto their lord all that was done. Then his lord, after that he had called him, said unto him, 'O thou wicked servant, I forgave thee all that debt, because

*Jesus here extends the power he gave to Peter to all the disciples, see p. 93.

thou desiredst me: shouldest not thou also have had compassion on thy fellowservant, even as I had pity on thee?' And his lord was wroth, and delivered him to the tormentors, till he should pay all that was due unto him. So likewise shall my heavenly Father do also unto you, if ye from your hearts forgive not every one his brother their trespasses."

And John answered him, saying, "Master, we saw one casting out devils in thy name, and he followeth not us: and we forbad him, because he followeth not us." But Jesus said, "Forbid him not: for there is no man which shall do a miracle in my name, that can lightly speak evil of me. For he that is not against us is on our part.* For whosoever shall give you a cup of water to drink in my name, because ye belong to Christ, verily I say unto you, he shall not lose his reward."

JESUS SENDS FORTH SEVENTY DISCIPLES

After these things the Lord appointed other seventy also, and sent them two and two before his face into every city and place, whither he himself would come. "Go your ways: behold, I send you forth as lambs among wolves. Carry neither purse, nor scrip, nor shoes: and salute no man by the way.† And into whatsoever house ye enter, first say, 'Peace *be* to this house.' And if the son of peace be there, your peace shall rest upon it; if not, it shall turn to you again. And in the same house remain, eating and drinking such things as they give: for the labourer is worthy of his hire. Go not from house to house. And into whatsoever city ye enter, and they receive you, eat such things as are set before you: and heal the sick that are therein, and say unto them, 'The kingdom of God is come nigh unto you.' But into

---

*Jesus is not disagreeing with his earlier statement, see p. 47. He is creating what in logic is called congruent classes.

†Naturally Jesus repeats many of his statements on sending the twelve, see p. 78.

whatsoever city ye enter, and they receive you not, go your ways out into the streets of the same, and say, 'Even the very dust of your city, which cleaveth on us, we do wipe off against you: notwithstanding be ye sure of this, that the kingdom of God is come nigh unto you.' He that heareth you heareth me; and he that despiseth you despiseth me; and he that despiseth me despiseth him that sent me."

And the seventy returned again with joy, saying, "Lord, even the devils are subject unto us through thy name." And he said unto them, "I beheld Satan as lightning fall from heaven. Behold, I give unto you power to tread on serpents and scorpions, and over all the power of the enemy: and nothing shall by any means hurt you. Notwithstanding in this rejoice not, that the spirits are subject unto you; but rather rejoice, because your names are written in heaven." In that hour Jesus rejoiced in spirit, and said, "I thank thee, O Father, Lord of heaven and earth, that thou hast hid these things from the wise and prudent, and hast revealed them unto babes: even so, Father; for so it seemed good in thy sight. All things are delivered to me of my Father: and no man knoweth who the Son is, but the Father; and who the Father is, but the Son, and *he* to whom the Son will reveal *him*." And he turned him unto *his* disciples, and said privately, "Blessed *are* the eyes which see the things that ye see: for I tell you, that many prophets and kings have desired to see those things which ye see, and have not seen *them*; and to hear those things which ye hear, and have not heard *them*."

JESUS HEADS FOR JERUSALEM

And it came to pass, when the time was come that he should be received up, he steadfastly set his face to go to Jerusalem, and he departed from Galilee, and came into the coasts of Judaea beyond Jordan; and great multitudes followed him; and he healed them there: and sent messengers before his face: and they went, and entered into a village of the Samaritans, to make ready for him. And they did not receive him, because his face was as though he would go to Jerusalem. And when his disciples James and John saw *this*, they said, "Lord, wilt thou that we command fire to come down from heaven, and consume them, even as Elias did?" But he turned, and rebuked them, and said, "Ye know not what manner of spirit ye are of. For the Son of man is not come to destroy men's lives, but to save *them*." And they went to another village.

HEALING OF THE SAMARITAN LEPER

And it came to pass, as he went to Jerusalem, that he passed through the midst of Samaria and Galilee. And as he entered into a certain village, there met him ten men that were lepers, which stood afar off: and they lifted up *their* voices, and said, "Jesus, Master, have mercy on us." And when he saw *them*, he said unto them, "Go shew yourselves unto the priests." And it came to pass, that, as they went, they were cleansed. And one of them, when he saw that he was healed, turned back, and with a loud voice glorified God, and fell down on *his* face at his feet, giving thanks: and he was a Samaritan. And Jesus answering said, "Were there not ten cleansed? but where *are* the nine? There are not found that returned to give glory to God, save this stranger." And he said unto him, "Arise, go thy way: thy faith hath made thee whole."

THE GOOD SAMARITAN

And, behold, a certain lawyer stood up, and tempted him, saying, "Master, what shall I do to inherit eternal life?"* He said

---

*For a similar statement on the law, see Jesus' statement during his last week, see p. 136.

unto him, "What is written in the law? how readest thou?" And he answering said, "Thou shalt love the Lord thy God with all thy heart, and with all thy soul, and with all thy strength, and with all thy mind; and thy neighbour as thyself." And he said unto him, "Thou hast answered right: this do, and thou shalt live." But he, willing to justify himself, said unto Jesus, "And who is my neighbour?" And Jesus answering said, "A certain man went down from Jerusalem to Jericho, and fell among thieves, which stripped him of his raiment, and wounded *him*, and departed, leaving *him* half dead. And by chance there came down a certain priest that way: and when he saw him, he passed by on the other side. And likewise a Levite, when he was at the place, came and looked *on him*, and passed by on the other side. But a certain Samaritan, as he journeyed, came where he was: and when he saw him, he had compassion *on him*. And went to *him*, and bound up his wounds, pouring in oil and wine, and set him on his own beast, and brought him to an inn, and took care of him. And on the morrow, when he departed, he took out two pence, and gave *them* to the host, and said unto him, 'Take care of him; and whatsoever thou spendest more, when I come again, I will repay thee.' Which now of these three, thinkest thou, was neighbour unto him that fell among the thieves?" And he said, "He that shewed mercy on him." Then said Jesus unto him, "Go, and do thou likewise."

ATTACKS THE PHARISEES AND LAWYERS

And as he spake, a certain Pharisee besought him to dine with him: and he went in, and sat down to meat. And when the Pharisee saw *it*, he marvelled that he had not first washed before dinner. And the Lord said unto him, "Now do ye Pharisees make clean the outside of the cup and the platter; but your inward part is full of ravening and wickedness. Ye fools, did not he that made that which is without make that which is within also? But rather give alms of such things as ye have; and, behold, all things are clean unto you. Woe unto you, Pharisees! for ye love the uppermost seats in the synagogues, and greetings in the markets. Woe unto you, scribes and Pharisees, hypocrites! for ye are as graves which appear not, and the men that walk over *them* are not aware *of them*."

Then answered one of the lawyers, and said unto him, "Master, thus saying thou reproachest us also." And he said, "Woe unto you also, *ye* lawyers! for ye lade men with burdens grievous to be borne, and ye yourselves touch not the burdens with one of your fingers. Woe unto you, lawyers! for ye have taken away the key of knowledge: ye entered not in yourselves, and them that were entering in ye hindered." And as he said these things unto them, the scribes and the Pharisees began to urge *him* vehemently, and to provoke him to speak of many things: laying wait for him, and seeking to catch something out of his mouth, that they might accuse him.

PARABLE OF THE RICH MAN

In the mean time, when there were gathered together an innumerable multitude of people, insomuch that they trode one upon another, one of the company said unto him, "Master, speak to my brother, that he divide the inheritance with me." And he said unto him, "Man, who made me a judge or a divider over you?" And he said unto them, "Take heed, and beware of covetousness: for a man's life consisteth not in the abundance of the things which he possesseth." And he spake a parable unto them, saying, "The ground of a certain rich man brought forth plentifully: and he thought within himself, saying, 'What shall I do, because I have no room where to bestow my fruits?' And he said, 'This will I do: I will pull down my barns, and build greater; and there will I bestow all my fruits and my goods. And I will say to my soul, "Soul, thou hast much goods laid up for many years; take thine ease, eat, drink, *and* be merry." ' But God said unto him, 'Thou fool, this night thy soul shall be required of thee: then whose shall those things be, which thou hast provided?' So *is* he that layeth up treasure for himself, and is not rich toward God. Fear not, little flock; for it is your Father's good pleasure to give you the kingdom. Sell that ye have, and give alms; provide yourselves bags which wax not old, a treasure in the heavens that faileth not. For where your treasure is, there will your heart be also. Let your loins be girded about, and *your* lights burning; and ye yourselves like unto men that wait for their lord, when he will return from the wedding; that when he cometh and knocketh, they may open unto him immediately. Blessed *are* those servants, whom the lord when he cometh shall find watching: verily I say unto you, that he shall gird himself, and make them to sit down to meat, and will come forth and serve them. And if he shall come in the second watch, or come in the third watch, and find *them* so, blessed are those servants.

"I am come to send fire on the earth: and what will I, if it be already kindled? But I have a baptism to be baptized with; and how am I straitened till it be accomplished! When ye see a cloud rise out of the west, straightway ye say, 'There cometh a shower'; and so it is. And when *ye see* the south wind blow, ye say, 'There will be heat'; and it cometh to pass. When it is evening, ye say, 'It *will be* fair weather: for the sky is red.' And in the morning, 'It *will be* foul weather today: for the sky is red and lowring.' O *ye* hypocrites, ye can discern the face of the sky and of the earth: but how is it that ye can not discern the signs of this time? Yea, and why even of yourselves judge ye not what is right?"

"DEGREE" OF SIN

There were present at that season some that told him of the Galilaeans, whose blood Pilate had mingled with their sacrifices. And Jesus answering said unto them, "Suppose ye that these

Galilaeans were sinners above all the Galilaeans, because they suffered such things? I tell you, Nay: but, except ye repent, ye shall all likewise perish. Or those eighteen, upon whom the tower in Siloam fell, and slew them, think ye that they were sinners above all men that dwelt in Jerusalem? I tell you, Nay: but, except ye repent, ye shall all likewise perish." He spake also this parable: "A certain *man* had a fig tree planted in his vineyard; and he came and sought fruit thereon, and found none. Then said he unto the dresser of his vineyard, "Behold, these three years I come seeking fruit on this fig tree, and find none: cut it down; why cumbereth it the ground?" And he answering said unto him, 'Lord, let it alone this year also, till I shall dig about it, and dung *it:* and if it bear fruit, *well:* and if not, *then* after that thou shalt cut it down.' "

HEALS THE ARTHRITIC WOMAN

And he was teaching in one of the synagogues on the sabbath, and, behold, there was a woman which had a spirit of infirmity eighteen years, and was bowed together, and could in no wise lift up *herself.* And when Jesus saw her, he called *her to him*, and said unto her, "Woman, thou art loosed from thine infirmity." And he laid *his* hands on her: and immediately she was made straight, and glorified God. And the ruler of the synagogue answered with indignation, because Jesus had healed on the sabbath day, and said unto the people, "There are six days in which men ought to work: in them therefore come and be healed, and not on the sabbath day." The Lord then answered him, and said, "Thou hypocrite, doth not each one of you on the sabbath loose his ox or *his* ass from the stall, and lead *him* away to watering? And ought not this woman, being a daughter of Abraham, whom Satan hath bound, lo, these eighteen years, be loosed from this bond on the sabbath day?"*

---

*This is quite a different illustration from the apparently similar one on p. 35.

And when he had said these things, all his adversaries were ashamed: and all the people rejoiced for all the glorious things that were done by him. And he went through the cities and villages, teaching, and journeying toward Jerusalem.

ENTER IN AT THE STRAIT GATE

Then said one unto him, "Lord, are there few that be saved?" And he said unto them, "Strive to enter in at the strait gate: for many, I say unto you, will seek to enter in, and shall not be able.* When once the master of the house is risen up, and hath shut to the door, and ye begin to stand without, and to knock at the door, saying, 'Lord, Lord, open unto us'; and he shall answer and say unto you, 'I know you not whence ye are': then shall ye begin to say, 'We have eaten and drunk in thy presence, and thou hast taught in our streets.' But he shall say, 'I tell you, I know you not whence ye are: depart from me, all *ye* workers of iniquity.' There shall be weeping and gnashing of teeth, when ye shall see Abraham, and Isaac, and Jacob, and all the prophets, in the kingdom of God, and you *yourselves* thrust out. And they shall come from the east, and *from* the west, and from the north, and *from* the south, and shall sit down in the kingdom of God. And, behold, there are many that are last which shall be first, and there are first which shall be last."†

PARABLE OF THE WEDDING FEAST

And he put forth a parable to those which were bidden, when he marked how they chose out the chief rooms; saying unto them, "When thou art bidden of any *man* to a wedding, sit not

---

*The context of this remark on the strait gate is quite different from p. 44.
†See a similar use of this statement on p. 97.

down in the highest room: lest a more honourable man than thou be bidden of him; and he that bade thee and him come and say to thee, 'Give this man place,' and thou begin with shame to take the lowest room. But when thou art bidden, go and sit down in the lowest room; that when he that bade thee cometh, he may say unto thee, 'Friend, go up higher': then shall thou have worship in the presence of them that sit at meat with thee. For whosoever exalteth himself shall be abased; and he that humbleth himself shall be exalted."

Then said he also to him that bade him, "When thou makest a dinner or a supper, call not thy friends, nor thy brethren, neither thy kinsmen, nor thy rich neighbours: lest they also bid thee again, and a recompence be made thee. But when thou makest a feast, call the poor, the maimed, the lame, and blind: and thou shalt be blessed; for they cannot recompense thee: for thou shalt be recompensed at the resurrection of the just." And when one of them that sat at meat with him heard these things, he said unto him, "Blessed is he that shall eat bread in the kingdom of God." Then said he unto him, "A certain man made a great supper, and bade many: and sent forth his servant at supper time to say to them that were bidden, 'Come: for all things are now ready.' And they all with one *consent* began to make excuse. The first said unto him, 'I have bought a piece of ground, and I must needs go and see it: I pray thee have me excused.' And another said, 'I have bought five yoke of oxen, and I go to prove them: I pray thee have me excused.' And another said, 'I have married a wife, and therefore I cannot come.' So that servant came, and shewed his lord these things. Then the master of the house being angry said to his servant, 'Go out quickly into the streets and lanes of the city, and bring in hither the poor, and the maimed, and the halt, and the blind.' And the servant said, 'Lord, it is done as thou hast commanded, and yet there is room.' And the lord said unto the servant, 'Go out into the highways and hedges, and compel *them* to come in, that my house may be filled. For I say unto you, That none of those men which were bidden shall taste of my supper.' "

FOLLOWING HIM

And there went great multitudes with him: and he turned, and said unto them, "If any *man* come to me, and hate not his father, and mother, and wife, and children, and brethren, and sisters, yea, and his own life also, he cannot be my disciple. And whosoever doth not bear his cross, and come after me, cannot be my disciple. For which of you, intending to build a tower, sitteth not down first, and counteth the cost, whether he have *sufficient* to finish *it?* Lest haply, after he hath laid the foundation, and is not able to finish *it,* all that behold *it* begin to mock him, saying, 'This man began to build, and was not able to finish.' Or what king, going to make war against another king, sitteth not down first, and consulteth whether he be able with ten thousand to meet him that cometh against him with twenty thousand? Or else, while the other is yet a great way off, he sendeth an ambassage, and desireth conditions of peace. So likewise, whosoever he be of you that forsaketh not all that he hath, he cannot be my disciple."

PARABLES OF THE LOST

Then drew near unto him all the publicans and sinners for to hear him. And the Pharisees and scribes murmured, saying, "This man receiveth sinners, and eateth with them." And he spake this parable unto them, saying, "What man of you, having an hundred sheep, if he lose one of them, doth not leave the ninety and nine in the wilderness, and go after that which is lost, until he find it? And when he hath found *it,* he layeth *it* on his shoulders, rejoicing. And when he cometh home, he calleth together *his* friends, and neighbours, saying unto them, 'Rejoice with me; for I have found my sheep which was lost.' I say unto you, that likewise joy shall be in heaven over one sinner that repenteth, more than over ninety and nine just persons, which need no repentance.*

"Either what woman having ten pieces of silver, if she lose one piece, doth not light a candle, and sweep the house, and seek diligently till she find *it?* And when she hath found *it*, she calleth *her* friends and *her* neighbours together, saying, 'Rejoice with me; for I have found the piece which I had lost.' Likewise, I say unto you there is joy in the presence of the angels of God over one sinner that repenteth.

THE PRODIGAL SON

And he said, "A certain man had two sons: and the younger of them said to *his* father, 'Father, give me the portion of goods that falleth *to me*.' And he divided unto them *his* living. And not many days after the younger son gathered all together, and took his journey into a far country, and there wasted his substance with riotous living. And when he had spent all, there arose a mighty famine in that land; and he began to be in want. And he went and joined himself to a citizen of that country; and he sent him into his fields to feed swine. And he would fain have filled his belly with the husks that the swine did eat: and no man gave unto him. And when he came to himself, he said, 'How many hired servants of my father's have bread enough and to spare, and I perish with hunger! I will arise and go to my father, and will say unto him, "Father, I have sinned against heaven, and before thee, and am no more worthy to be called thy son: make me as one of thy hired servants." ' And he arose, and came to his father. But when he was yet a great way off, his father saw him, and had compassion, and ran, and fell on his neck, and kissed him. And the son said unto him, 'Father, I have sinned

*Jesus repeats the parable he spoke to his disciples a bit earlier for a larger group of listeners and emphasizes his point with another parable, see p. 98.

against heaven, and in thy sight, and am no more worthy to be called thy son.' But the father said to his servants, 'Bring forth the best robe, and put *it* on him; and put a ring on his hand, and shoes on *his* feet: and bring hither the fatted calf, and kill *it*; and let us eat, and be merry: for this my son was dead, and is alive again; he was lost, and is found.' And they began to be merry. Now his elder son was in the field: and as he came and drew nigh to the house, he heard musick and dancing. And he called one of the servants, and asked what these things meant. And he said unto him, 'Thy brother is come; and thy father hath killed the fatted calf, because he hath received him safe and sound.' And he was angry, and would not go in: therefore came his father out, and intreated him. And he answering said to *his* father, 'Lo, these many years do I serve thee, neither transgressed I at any time thy commandment: and yet thou never gavest me a kid, that I might make merry with my friends: but as soon as this thy son was come, which hath devoured thy living with harlots, thou hast killed for him the fatted calf.' And he said unto him, 'Son, thou art ever with me, and all that I have is thine. It was meet that we should make merry, and be glad: for this thy brother was dead, and is alive again; and was lost, and is found.' "

THE UNJUST SERVANT

And he said also unto his disciples, "There was a certain rich man, which had a steward; and the same was accused unto him that he had wasted his goods. And he called him, and said unto him, 'How is it that I hear this of thee? give an account of thy stewardship; for thou mayest be no longer steward.' Then the steward said within himself, 'What shall I do? for my lord taketh away from me the stewardship: I cannot dig; to beg I am ashamed. I am resolved what to do, that, when I am put out of the stewardship, they may receive me into their houses.' So he called every one of his lord's debtors *unto him*, and said unto the first, 'How much owest thou unto my lord?' And he said, 'An hundred measures of oil.' And he said unto him, 'Take thy bill, and sit down quickly, and write fifty.' Then said he to another, 'And how much owest thou?' And he said, 'An hundred measures of wheat.' And he said unto him, 'Take thy bill, and write fourscore.' And the lord commended the unjust steward, because he had done wisely: for the children of this world are in their generation wiser than the children of light. And I say unto you, Make to yourselves friends of the mammon of unrighteousness: that, when ye fail, they may receive you into everlasting habitations. He that is faithful in that which is least is faithful also in much; and he that is unjust in the least is unjust also in much. If therefore ye have not been faithful in the unrighteous mammon, who will commit to your trust the true *riches?* And if ye have not been faithful in that which is another man's, who shall give you that which is your own?" And the Pharisees also, who were covetous, heard all these things: and they derided him. And he said unto them, "Ye are they which justify yourselves before men; but God knoweth your hearts: for that which is highly esteemed among men is abomination in the sight of God.

THE RICH MAN AND LAZARUS

"There was a certain rich man, which was clothed in purple and fine linen, and fared sumptuously every day: and there was a certain beggar named Lazarus, which was laid at his gate, full of sores, and desiring to be fed with the crumbs which fell from the rich man's table: moreover the dogs came and licked his sores. And it came to pass, that the beggar died, and was carried by the angels into Abraham's bosom: the rich man also died, and was buried; and in hell he lift up his eyes, being in torments, and seeth Abraham afar off, and Lazarus in his bosom. And he cried and said, 'Father Abraham, have mercy on me, and send Lazarus, that he may dip the tip of his finger in water, and cool my tongue; for I am tormented in this flame.' But Abraham said, 'Son, remember that thou in thy lifetime receivedst thy good things, and likewise Lazarus evil things: but now he is comforted and thou art tormented. And beside all this, between us and you there is a great gulf fixed: so that they which would pass from hence to you cannot; neither can they pass to us, that *would come* from thence.' Then he said, 'I pray thee therefore, father, that thou wouldest send him to my father's house: for I have five brethren; that he may testify unto them, lest they also come into this place of torment.' Abraham saith unto him, 'They have Moses and the prophets: let them hear them.' And he said, 'Nay, father Abraham: but if one went unto them from the dead, they will repent.' And he said unto him, 'If they hear not Moses and the prophets, neither will they be persuaded, though one rose from the dead.'

"Take heed to yourselves: If thy brother trespass against thee, rebuke him; and if he repent, forgive him. And if he trespass against thee seven times in a day, and seven times in a day turn again to thee, saying, 'I repent'; thou shalt forgive him." And the apostles said unto the Lord, "Increase our faith." And the Lord said, "If ye had faith as a grain of mustard seed, ye might say unto this sycamine tree, 'Be thou plucked up by the root, and be thou planted in the sea'; and it should obey you.*

"But which of you, having a servant plowing or feeding cattle, will say unto him by and by, when he is come from the field, 'Go and sit down to meat?' And will not rather say unto him, 'Make ready wherewith I may sup, and gird thyself, and serve me, till I have eaten and drunken; and afterward thou shalt eat and drink?' Doth he thank that servant because he did the things that were commanded him? I trow not. So likewise ye, when ye shall have done all those things which are commanded you, say, 'We are unprofitable servants: we have done that which was our duty to do.' "

*See parallel statement on p. 96 and the union of the two examples on p. 131.

THE COMING OF THE KINGDOM

And when he was demanded of the Pharisees, when the kingdom of God should come, he answered them and said, "The kingdom of God cometh not with observation: neither shall they say, 'Lo here!' or, 'lo there!' for, behold, the kingdom of God is within you." And he said unto the disciples, "The days will come, when ye shall desire to see one of the days of the Son of man, and ye shall not see *it*. And they shall say to you, 'See here'; or, 'see there': go not after *them*, nor follow *them*. But first must he suffer many things, and be rejected of this generation. And as it was in the days of Noe, so shall it be also in the days of the Son of man. They did eat, they drank, they married wives, they were given in marriage, until the day that Noe entered into the ark, and the flood came, and destroyed them all. Likewise also as it was in the days of Lot; they did eat, they drank, they bought, they sold, they planted, they builded; but the same day that Lot went out of Sodom it rained fire and brimstone from heaven, and destroyed *them* all. Even thus shall it be in the day when the Son of man is revealed. In that day, he which shall be upon the housetop, and his stuff in the house, let him not come down to take it away: and he that is in the field, let him likewise not return back. Remember Lot's wife. Whosoever shall seek to save his life shall lose it; and whosoever shall lose his life shall preserve it.* I tell you, in that night there shall be two *men* in one bed; and one shall be taken, and the other shall be left. Two *women* shall be grinding together; one shall be taken, and the other left. Two *men* shall be in the field; the one shall be taken, and the other left." And they answered and said unto him, "Where, Lord?" And he said unto them, 'Wheresoever the body *is*, thither will the eagles be gathered together."

*Obviously one of Jesus' favorite warnings, it appears on pp. 80, 93, and 127.

PARABLE OF THE UNJUST JUDGE

And he spake a parable unto them *to this end,* that men ought always to pray, and not to faint; saying, "There was in a city a judge, which feared not God, neither regarded man: and there was a widow in that city; and she came unto him, saying, 'Avenge me of mine adversary.' And he would not for a while: but afterward he said within himself, 'Though I fear not God, nor regard man; yet because this widow troubleth me, I will avenge her, lest by her continual coming she weary me.' " And the Lord said, "Hear what the unjust judge saith. And shall not God avenge his own elect, which cry day and night unto him, though he bear long with them? I tell you that he will avenge them speedily. Nevertheless when the Son of man cometh, shall he find faith on the earth?"

And he spake this parable unto certain which trusted in themselves that they were righteous, and despised others: "Two men went up into the temple to pray; the one a Pharisee, and the other a publican. The Pharisee stood and prayed thus with himself, 'God, I thank thee, that I am not as other men *are,* extortioners, unjust, adulterers, or even as this publican. I fast twice in the week. I give tithes of all that I possess.' And the publican, standing afar off, would not lift up so much as *his* eyes unto heaven, but smote upon his breast, saying, 'God, be merciful to me a sinner.' I tell you, this man went down to his house justified *rather* than the other: for every one that exalteth himself shall be abased; and he that humbleth himself shall be exalted."

THE RAISING OF LAZARUS

Now a certain *man* was sick, *named* Lazarus, of Bethany, the town of Mary and her sister Martha. (It was *that* Mary which anointed the Lord with ointment, and wiped his feet with her hair, whose brother Lazarus was sick.) Therefore his sisters sent unto him, saying, "Lord, behold, he whom thou lovest is sick." When Jesus heard *that*, he said, "This sickness is not unto death, but for the glory of God, that the Son of God might be glorified thereby." Now Jesus loved Martha, and her sister, and Lazarus. When he had heard therefore that he was sick, he abode two days still in the same place where he was. Then after that saith he to *his* disciples, "Let us go into Judaea again." *His* disciples say unto him, "Master, the Jews of late sought to stone thee; and goest thou thither again?" Jesus answered, "Are there not twelve hours in the day? If any man walk in the day, he stumbleth not, because he seeth the light of this world. But if a man walk in the night, he stumbleth, because there is no light in him." These things said he: and after that he saith unto them, "Our friend Lazarus sleepeth; but I go, that I may awake him out of sleep." Then said his disciples, "Lord, if he sleep, he shall do well." Howbeit Jesus spake of his death: but they thought that he had spoken of taking of rest in sleep. Then said Jesus unto them plainly, "Lazarus is dead. And I am glad for your sakes that I was not there, to the intent ye may believe; nevertheless let us go unto him." Then said Thomas, which is called Didymus, unto his fellowdisciples, "Let us also go, that we may die with him." Then when Jesus came, he found that he had *lain* in the grave four days already.

Now Bethany was nigh unto Jerusalem, about fifteen furlongs off: and many of the Jews came to Martha and Mary, to comfort them concerning their brother. Then Martha, as soon as she heard that Jesus was coming, went and met him: but Mary sat *still* in the house. Then said Martha unto Jesus, "Lord, if thou hadst been here, my brother had not died. But I know, that even now, whatsoever thou wilt ask of God, God will give *it* thee." Jesus saith unto her, "Thy brother shall rise again." Martha saith unto him, "I know that he shall rise again in the resurrection at the last day." Jesus said unto her, "I am the resurrection, and the life: he that believeth in me, though he were dead, yet shall he live: and whosoever liveth and believeth in me shall never die. Believest thou this?" She saith unto him, "Yea, Lord: I believe that thou art the Christ, the Son of God, which should come into the world." And when she had so said, she went her way, and called Mary her sister secretly, saying, "The Master is come, and calleth for thee." As soon as she heard *that*, she arose quickly, and came unto him.

Now Jesus was not yet come into the town, but was in that place where Martha met him. The Jews then which were with her in the house, and comforted her, when they saw Mary, that she rose up hastily and went out, followed her, saying, "She goeth unto the grave to weep there." Then when Mary was come where Jesus was, and saw him, she fell down at his feet, saying unto him, "Lord, if thou hadst been here, my brother had not died." When Jesus therefore saw her weeping, and the Jews also weeping which came with her, he groaned in the spirit, and was troubled, and said, "Where have ye laid him?" They said unto him, "Lord, come and see." Jesus wept. Then said the Jews, "Behold how he loved him!" And some of them said, "Could not this man, which opened the eyes of the blind, have caused that even this man should not have died?" Jesus therefore again groaning in himself cometh to the grave. It was a cave, and a stone lay upon it. Jesus said, "Take ye away the stone." Martha, the sister of him that was dead, saith unto him, "Lord, by this time he stinketh: for he hath been *dead* four days." Jesus saith unto her, "Said I not unto thee, that, if thou wouldest believe, thou shouldest see the glory of God?" Then they took away the stone *from the place* where the dead was laid. And Jesus lifted up *his* eyes, and said, "Father, I thank thee that thou hast heard me. And I knew that thou hearest me always: but because of the people which stand by I said *it*, that they may believe that thou hast sent me." And when he thus had spoken he cried with a loud voice, "Lazarus, come forth." And he that was dead came forth, bound hand and foot with graveclothes: and his face was bound about with a napkin. Jesus saith unto them, "Loose him, and let him go." Then many of the Jews which came to Mary, and had seen the things which Jesus did, believed on him. But some of them went their ways to the Pharisees, and told them what things Jesus had done.

THE COUNCIL PLOTS JESUS' DEATH

Then gathered the chief priests and the Pharisees a council, and said, "What do we? for this man doeth many miracles. If we let him thus alone, all *men* will believe on him: and the Romans shall come and take away both our place and nation." And one of them, *named* Caiaphas, being the high priest that same year, said unto them, "Ye know nothing at all, nor consider that it is expedient for us, that one man should die for the people, and that the whole nation perish not." And this spake he not of himself: but being high priest that year, he prophesied that Jesus should die for that nation: and not for that nation only, but that also he should gather together in one the children of God that were scattered abroad. Then from that day forth they took counsel together for to put him to death. Jesus therefore walked no more openly among the Jews; but went thence unto a country near to the wilderness, into a city called Ephraim, and there continued with his disciples.

MARRIAGE AND DIVORCE

And the people resort unto him again; and, as he was wont, he taught them again. The Pharisees also came unto him, tempting him, and saying unto him, "Is it lawful for a man to put away his wife for every cause?" And he answered and said unto them, "What did Moses command you?" They said unto him, "Moses suffered to write a bill of divorcement, and to put her away." And Jesus answered and said unto them, "Moses because of the hardness of your hearts wrote you this precept and suffered you to put away your wives: but from the beginning it was not so. Have ye not read that God which made *them* from the beginning of the creation made them male and female. For this cause shall a man leave his father and mother, and shall cleave to his wife; and they twain shall be one flesh? Wherefore they are no more twain, but one flesh. What therefore God hath joined together, let no man put asunder." And in the house his disciples asked him again of the same *matter*. And he saith unto them, "I say unto you, Whosoever shall put away his wife, except *it be* for fornication, and shall marry another, committeth adultery against her: and whoso marrieth her which is put away, doth commit adultery. And if a woman shall put away her husband, and be married to another, she committeth adultery."* His disciples say unto him, "If the case of the man be so with *his* wife, it is not good to marry." But he said unto them, "All *men* cannot receive this saying, save *they* to whom it is given. For there are some eunuchs, which were so born from *their* mother's womb: and there are some eunuchs, which were made eunuchs of men: and there be eunuchs, which have made themselves eunuchs for the kingdom of heaven's sake. He that is able to receive *it*, let him receive *it*."

BLESSES LITTLE CHILDREN

Then they brought little children [infants—Luke] unto him that he should put *his* hands on them, and pray: but when *his* disciples saw *it*, they rebuked those that brought *them*. But when Jesus saw *it*, he was much displeased *and* called them *unto him*, and said, "Suffer the little children to come unto me, and forbid them not: for of such is the kingdom of God [heaven—Mat-

*Only the conclusion of this statement on divorce repeats the passage in the Sermon on the Mount, see p. 39. The fuller statement is much more important.

thew]. Verily I say unto you, Whosoever shall not receive the kingdom of God as a little child, he shall in no wise enter therein." And he took them up in his arms, put *his* hands upon them, and blessed them.

THE RICH YOUNG RULER

And when he was departed thence, and gone forth into the way, there came a certain ruler running, and kneeled to him, and said unto him, "Good Master, what good thing shall I do that I may inherit eternal life?" And Jesus said unto him, "Why callest thou me good? *There is* none good but one, *that is*, God: but if thou wilt enter into life, keep the commandments." He saith unto him, "Which?" Jesus said, "Thou knowest the commandments, "Thou shalt not kill, Thou shalt not commit adultery, Thou shalt not steal, Thou shalt not bear false witness, Defraud not, Honour thy father and thy mother: and, thou shalt love thy neighbour as thyself." The young man answered and said unto him, "Master, all these things have I kept from my youth up: what lack I yet?" Now when he heard these things, Jesus beholdeth him, loved him, and said unto him, "Yet one thing thou lackest, if thou wilt be perfect: go thy way and sell all that thou hast, and distribute unto the poor, and thou shalt have treasure in heaven: and come, take up the cross, and follow me." And when the young man heard that saying, he was very sorrowful, and went away grieved: for he was very rich *and* had great possessions. And when Jesus saw that he was very sorrowful, he looked round about, and saith unto his disciples, "Verily I say unto you, How hardly shall they that have riches enter into the kingdom of God." And the disciples were astonished at his words. But Jesus answereth again, and saith unto them, "Children, again I say unto you, how hard is it for them that trust in riches to enter into the kingdom of God! It is easier for a camel to go through the eye of a needle, than for a rich man to enter into the kingdom of God." When his disciples heard *it*, they were exceedingly amazed out of measure, saying among themselves, "Who then can be saved?" And Jesus looking upon them saith unto them, "With men this is impossible, but not with God: for with God all things are possible."

THE DISCIPLES AS JUDGES OF ISRAEL

Then Peter began to say unto him, "Behold, we have forsaken all, and have followed thee; what shall we have therefore?" And Jesus answered and said unto them, "Verily I say unto you, That ye which have followed me, and continued with me in my temptations I *shall* appoint unto you a kingdom, as my Father hath appointed unto me; that ye may eat and drink at my table in my kingdom, and in the regeneration when the Son of man shall sit in the throne of his glory, ye also shall sit upon twelve thrones, judging the twelve tribes of Israel. There is no man that hath left house, or brethren, or sisters, or father, or mother, or wife, or children, or lands for my name's sake [kingdom of God's sake—Luke], and the gospel's, but he shall receive an hundredfold now in this time, houses, and brethren, and sisters, and mothers, and children, and lands, with persecutions: and in the world to come everlasting life.

PARABLES OF THE LABOURERS IN THE VINEYARD

"For the kingdom of heaven is like unto a man *that is* an householder, which went out early in the morning to hire labourers into his vineyard. And when he had agreed with the labourers for a penny a day, he sent them into his vineyard. And he went out about the third hour, and saw others standing idle in the marketplace, and said unto them: 'Go ye also into the vineyard, and whatsoever is right I will give you.' And they went their way. Again he went out about the sixth and ninth hour, and did likewise. And about the eleventh hour he went out, and found others standing idle, and saith unto them, 'Why stand ye here all the day idle?' They say unto him, 'Because no man hath hired us.' He saith unto them, 'Go ye also into the vineyard: and whatsoever is right, *that* shall ye receive.' So when even was come, the lord of the vineyard saith unto his steward, 'Call the labourers, and give them *their* hire, beginning from the last unto the first.' And when they came that *were hired* about the eleventh hour, they received every man a penny. But when the first came, they supposed that they should have received more; and they likewise received every man a penny. And when they had received *it*, they murmured against the goodman of the house, saying, "These last have wrought *but* one hour, and thou hast made them equal unto us, which have borne the burden and heat of the day.' But he answered one of them and said, 'Friend, I do thee no wrong: didst not thou agree with me for a penny? Take *that* thine *is*, and go thy way: I will give unto this last, even as unto thee. Is it not lawful for me to do what I will with mine own? Is thine eye evil, because I am good?' So the last shall be first, and the first last: for many be called, but few chosen."

THE DISCIPLES DISPUTE THEIR PLACE IN HEAVEN

And James and John, the sons of Zebedee, come unto him, saying, "Master, we would that thou shouldest do for us whatsoever we shall desire." And he said unto them, "What would ye that I should do for you?" They said unto him, "Grant unto us that we may sit, [Then came to him the mother of Zebedee's children with her sons, worshipping *him*, and desiring a certain thing of him. And he said unto her, "What wilt thou?" She saith unto him, "Grant that these my two sons may sit—Matthew] one on thy right hand, and the other on thy left hand, in thy glory." But Jesus said unto them, "Ye know not what ye ask: can ye drink of the cup that I drink of? and be baptized with the baptism that I am baptized with?" And they said unto him, "We can." And Jesus said unto them, "Ye shall indeed drink of the cup that I drink of; and with the baptism that I am baptized withal shall ye be baptized: but to sit on my right hand and on my left hand is not mine to give; but *it shall be given to them* for whom it is prepared of my Father." And when the ten heard *it*, they began to be much displeased with James and John. But Jesus called them to *him*, and saith unto them, "Ye know that they which are accounted kings of the Gentiles exercise lordship over them; and their great ones that exercise authority upon them are called benefactors. But so shall it not be among you: but whosoever will be greatest among you, let him be as the younger, he shall be your minister; and whosoever of you will be the chiefest, shall be servant of all.* For whether *is* greater, he that sitteth at meat, or he that serveth? is it not he that sitteth at meat? but I am among you as he that serveth. For even the Son of man came not to be ministered unto, but to minister, and to give his life a ransom for many."

VISITS ZACCHAEUS IN JERICHO

And Jesus entered and passed through Jericho. And, behold, *there was* a man named Zacchaeus, which was the chief among the publicans, and he was rich. And he sought to see Jesus who he was; and could not for the press, because he was little of stature. And he ran before, and climbed up into a sycomore tree to see him: for he was to pass that *way*. And when Jesus came to the place, he looked up, and saw him, and said unto him, "Zacchaeus, make haste, and come down; for today I must

*This passage repeats the general tenor of p. 97, where he discusses true discipleship. The request was perhaps triggered by the remarks on p. 121.

abide at thy house. And he made haste, and came down, and received him joyfully. And when they saw *it*, they all murmured, saying, "That he was gone to be a guest with a man that is a sinner." And Zacchaeus stood, and said unto the Lord: "Behold, Lord, the half of my goods I give to the poor: and if I have taken any thing from any man by false accusation, I restore *him* four-fold." And Jesus said unto him, "This day is salvation come to this house forsomuch as he also is a son of Abraham. For the Son of man is come to seek and to save that which was lost."*

CURES A BLIND MAN†

And as they departed from Jericho, a great multitude followed him with his disciples, and, behold, a certain blind man [two—Matthew], Bartimaeus, the son of Timaeus, sat by the highway side begging. And hearing the multitude pass by, he asked what it meant, and they told him that Jesus of Nazareth passeth by. And when he heard that it was Jesus *who* passed by, he cried out, saying, "Jesus [O Lord—Matthew], *thou* son of David, have mercy on me." And the multitude which went before rebuked him, that he should hold his peace: but he cried so much the more, "*Thou* son of David, have mercy on me." And Jesus stood still, and commanded him to be called *and* brought unto him: and they call the blind man, saying unto him, "Be of good comfort, rise; he calleth thee." And he, casting away his garment, rose, and came to Jesus: and when he was come near, Jesus answered and said unto him, "What wilt thou that I shall do unto thee?" The blind man said unto him, "Lord, that *my* eyes may be opened, that I may receive my sight." So Jesus had compassion, and touched *his* eyes, and said unto him, "Receive thy sight. Go thy way; thy faith hath made thee whole [saved

*See also p. 98.
†Luke places this miracle on the way into Jericho.

thee—Luke]." And immediately he received his sight, and followed Jesus in the way, glorifying God: and all the people, when they saw *it*, gave praise unto God. And when he had thus spoken he went before, ascending up to Jerusalem.

And the Jews' passover was nigh at hand: and many went out of the country up to Jerusalem before the passover, to purify themselves. Then sought they for Jesus, and spake among themselves, as they stood in the temple, "What think ye, that he will not come to the feast?" Now both the chief priests and the Pharisees had given a commandment, that, if any man knew where he were, he should shew *it*, that they might take him. Then Jesus six days before the passover came to Bethany, where Lazarus was which had been dead, whom he raised from the dead. There they made him a supper: and Martha served: but Lazarus was one of them that sat at the table with him. Much people of the Jews therefore knew that he was there: and they came not for Jesus' sake only, but that they might see Lazarus also, whom he had raised from the dead. But the chief priests consulted that they might put Lazarus also to death: because that by reason of him many of the Jews went away, and believed on Jesus.

PALM SUNDAY

On the next day, it came to pass, when they drew nigh unto Jerusalem, and were come to Bethphage, unto the mount of Olives, he sendeth forth two of his disciples, and saith unto them, "Go into the village over against you: and as soon as you be entered into it you shall find an ass and a colt tied with her, whereon yet never man sat: loose him and bring *him* [them— Matthew] unto me. And if any man say unto you, 'Why do ye this?' say ye, 'Because the Lord hath need of him' [them— Matthew]; and straightway he will send him hither." All this was done, that it might be fulfilled which was spoken by the prophet, saying, "Tell ye the daughter of Sion, 'Fear not; behold, thy king cometh unto thee, meek, and sitting upon an ass, and a colt the foal of an ass.' " These things understood not his disciples at the first: but when Jesus was glorified, then remembered they that these things were written of him, and *that* they had done these things unto him. And the disciples that were sent went their way, and found even as he had said unto them, and did as Jesus commanded them, and found the colt tied by the door without in a place where two ways met. And as they were loosing the colt, the owners thereof that stood there said unto them, "What do ye, why loose ye the colt?" And they said, "The Lord hath need of him," even as Jesus had commanded: and they let them go. And they brought the colt [and the ass—Matthew] to Jesus: and they cast their garments on the colt, and they set Jesus thereon.

And as he went many spread their garments in the way; others cut down branches from the trees, and strawed *them* in the way. And the multitudes that were come to the feast, when they heard that Jesus was coming to Jerusalem, took branches of palm trees, and went forth to meet him. And when he was come nigh, even now at the descent of the mount of Olives, the whole multitude of the disciples that went before, and that followed, began to rejoice and praise God with a loud voice for all the mighty works that they had seen, and cried, saying, "Hosanna to the son of David: Blessed *is* he that cometh in the name of the Lord: Blessed *is* the King of Israel, the kingdom of our father David, that cometh in the name of the Lord: peace in heaven, and glory in the highest: Hosanna in the highest."*

And some of the Pharisees from among the multitude said unto him, "Master, rebuke thy disciples." And he answered and said unto them, "I tell you that, if these should hold their peace, the stones would immediately cry out." And when he was come near, he beheld the city, and wept over it, saying, "If thou hadst known,

*The difference in wording from the message of the angels is significant, see p. 10.

even thou, at least in this thy day, the things *which belong* unto thy peace! but now they are hid from thine eyes. For the days shall come upon thee, that thine enemies shall cast a trench about thee, and compass thee round, and keep thee in on every side, and shall lay thee even with the ground, and thy children with thee; and they shall not leave in thee one stone upon another: because thou knewest not the time of thy visitation."

And when he was come into Jerusalem, all the city was moved, saying, "Who is this?" And the multitude said, "This is Jesus the prophet of Nazareth of Galilee." The people therefore that was with him when he called Lazarus out of his grave, and raised him from the dead, bare record. For this cause the people also met him, for that they heard that he had done this miracle. The Pharisees therefore said among themselves, "Perceive ye how ye prevail nothing? behold, the world is gone after him."

A VOICE FROM HEAVEN
GLORIFIES JESUS

And there were certain Greeks among them that came up to worship at the feast: the same came therefore to Philip, which was of Bethsaida of Galilee, and desired him saying, "Sir, we would see Jesus." Philip cometh and telleth Andrew: and again Andrew and Philip tell Jesus. And Jesus answered them, saying, "The hour is come, that the Son of man should be glorified. Verily, verily, I say unto you, Except a corn of wheat fall into the ground and die, it abideth alone: but if it die, it bringeth forth much fruit. He that loveth his life shall lose it; and he that hateth his life in this world shall keep it unto life eternal.* If any man serve me, let him follow me; and where I am, there shall also my servant be: if any man serve me, him will *my* Father honour. Now is my soul troubled; and what shall I say? 'Father, save me from this hour'; but for this cause came I unto this

*See p. 114.

hour. Father, glorify thy name." Then came there a voice from
heaven, *saying*, "I have both glorified *it*, and will glorify *it*
again." The people therefore, that stood by, and heard *it*, said
that it thundered: others said, "An angel spake to him." Jesus
answered and said, "This voice came not because of me, but for
your sakes. Now is the judgment of this world: now shall the
prince of this world be cast out. And I, if I be lifted up from the
earth, will draw all *men* unto me." This he said, signifying what
death he should die. The people answered him, "We have heard
out of the law that Christ abideth forever: and how sayest thou,
'The Son of man must be lifted up?' who is this Son of man?"
Then Jesus said unto them, "Yet a little while is the light with
you. Walk while ye have the light, lest darkness come upon you:
for he that walketh in darkness knoweth not whither he goeth.
While ye have the light, believe in the light, that ye may be the
children of light."

These things spake Jesus, and departed, and did hide himself
from them. But though he had done so many miracles before
them, yet they believed not on him: that the saying of Esaias the
prophet might be fulfilled, which he spake, "Lord, who hath
believed our report? and to whom hath the arm of the Lord
been revealed?" Therefore they could not believe, because that
Esaias said again, "He hath blinded their eyes, and hardened
their heart; that they should not see with *their* eyes, nor understand with *their* heart, and be converted, and I should heal
them."* These things said Esaias, when he saw his glory, and
spake of him. Nevertheless among the chief rulers also many
believed on him; but because of the Pharisees they did not confess *him*, lest they should be put out of the synagogue: for they
loved the praise of men more than the praise of God.

Jesus cried and said, "He that believeth on me, believeth not
on me, but on him that sent me. And he that seeth me seeth
him that sent me. I am come a light into the world, that whoso-

---

*The writer uses the same passage Jesus had used for the parables, see p. 68.

ever believeth on me should not abide in darkness.* And if any man hear my words, and believe not, I judge him not: for I came not to judge the world, but to save the world. He that rejecteth me, and receiveth not my words, hath one that judgeth him: the word that I have spoken, the same shall judge him in the last day. For I have not spoken of myself; but the Father which sent me, he gave me a commandment, what I should say, and what I should speak. And I know that his commandment is life everlasting: whatsoever I speak therefore, even as the Father said unto me, so I speak."

And Jesus entered into the temple: and when he had looked round about upon all things, and now the eventide was come, he went out unto Bethany with the twelve; and he lodged there.

MONDAY

And on the morrow, as he returned into the city, when they were come from Bethany, he was hungry: and seeing a fig tree in the way afar off having leaves, he came, if haply he might find anything thereon: and when he came to it, he found nothing but leaves: for the time of the figs was not *yet*. And Jesus answered and said unto it, "Let no fruit grow on thee *and* no man eat fruit of thee hereafter for ever." And his disciples heard it.[†]

And they come to Jerusalem: and Jesus went into the temple of God, and found in the temple those that sold oxen and sheep and doves, and the changers of money sitting: and when he had made a scourge of small cords, he began to cast out all of them that sold and bought in the temple, and drove them all out of

---

*Jesus may be remembering his earlier speech in the temple which contained many of the same ideas, see p. 62.

†Matthew has the fig tree wither immediately.

the temple, and the sheep, and the oxen; and poured out the changers' money, and overthrew the tables of the money changers, and the seats of them that sold doves; and would not suffer any man should carry *any* vessel through the temple. And he taught and said unto them that sold doves, "Take these things hence; make not my Father's house an house of merchandise. It is written, 'My house shall be called of all nations the house of prayer': but ye have made it a den of thieves." And his disciples remembered that it was written, "The zeal of thine house hath eaten me up." Then answered the Jews and said unto him, "What sign shewest thou unto us, seeing that thou doest these things?" Jesus answered and said unto them, "Destroy this temple, and in three days I will raise it up." Then said the Jews, "Forty and six years was this temple in building, and wilt thou rear it up in three days?" But he spake of the temple of his body. When therefore he was risen from the dead, his disciples remembered that he had said this unto them: and they believed the scripture, and the word which Jesus had said.

And the blind and the lame came to him in the temple; and he healed them. And when the chief priests and scribes saw the wonderful things that he did, and the children crying in the temple, and saying, "Hosanna to the son of David"; they were sore displeased, and said unto him, "Hearest thou what these say?" And Jesus saith unto them, "Yea; have ye never read, 'Out of the mouth of babes and sucklings thou hast perfected praise?' " And he taught daily in the temple, and the scribes and chief priests and the chiefs of the people heard *it*, and sought how they might destroy him: for they feared him, because all the people was astonished at his doctrine, and *they* could not find what they might do: for all the people were very attentive to hear him.

And when even was come, he went out of the city into Bethany.

TUESDAY

And in the morning, as they passed by, they saw the fig tree dried up from the roots. And when the disciples saw *it*, they marvelled, saying, "How soon is the fig tree withered away!" And Peter calling to remembrance saith unto him, "Master, behold, the fig tree which thou cursedst is withered away." Jesus answered and said unto them, "Have faith in God. For verily I say unto you, If ye have faith, and doubt not, ye shall not only do this *which is done* to the fig tree, but also if ye shall say unto this mountain, 'Be thou removed, and be thou cast into the sea'; and shall not doubt in *your* heart, but shall believe that those things shall come to pass, it shall be done: *you* shall have whatsoever *thou* saith.* Therefore I say unto you, What things soever ye desire, when ye pray, believe that ye receive *them,* and ye shall have *them.* And when ye stand praying, forgive, if ye have ought against any: that your Father also which is in heaven may forgive you your trespasses."

BY WHAT AUTHORITY?

And they come again to Jerusalem: and as he was walking in the temple, he taught the people and preached the gospel; and the chief priests, and the scribes, and the elders of the people came unto him as he was teaching, and said unto him, "Tell us, by what authority doest thou these things? and who gave thee this authority to do these things?" And Jesus answered and said unto them, "I will also ask of you one question, and answer me, and I will tell you by what authority I do these things. The baptism of John, whence was it? was *it* from heaven, or of men? answer me." And they reasoned with themselves, saying, "If we shall

*This passage joins two previous statements together, see pp. 96 and 113.

say, 'From heaven'; he will say, 'Why then did ye not believe him?' But if we shall say, 'Of men'; we fear the people will stone us: for all *men are* persuaded that John was a prophet indeed." And they answered and said unto Jesus, "We cannot tell." And Jesus answering saith unto them, "Neither do I tell you by what authority I do these things."

PARABLES OF THE VINEYARD

And he began to speak unto them by parables. "But what think ye? A *certain* man had two sons: and he came to the first, and said, 'Son, go work to day in my vineyard.' He answered and said, 'I will not': but afterward he repented, and went. And he came to the second, and said likewise. And he answered and said, 'I go, sir': and went not. Whether of them twain did the will of *his* father?" They say unto him, "The first." Jesus saith unto them, "Verily I say unto you, That the publicans and the harlots go into the kingdom of God before you. For John came unto you in the way of righteousness, and ye believed him not; but the publicans and the harlots believed him: and ye, when ye had seen *it*, repented not afterward, that ye might believe him.

"Hear another parable: There was a certain householder which planted a vineyard, and set an hedge round about it, and digged a winepress in it for the winefat, and built a tower, and let it out to husbandmen, and went into a far country for a long time. At the season when the time of the fruit drew near, he sent his servant to the husbandmen, that he might receive from the husbandmen of the fruit of the vineyard. And they caught *him*, and beat him, and sent *him* away empty. And again he sent unto them another servant; and at him they cast stones, and wounded *him* in the head, and sent *him* away again shamefully handled. And again he sent another; and him they killed, and many others: beating some, and killing some. Then said the lord of the vineyard, 'What shall I do?' Having yet therefore one son, his wellbeloved, he sent him also last unto them, saying, "It may be they will reverence my son.' But those husbandmen, when they saw him, said among themselves, 'This is the heir; come, let us kill him, and the inheritance shall be ours.' And they took him, and killed *him*, and cast *him* out of the vineyard. What shall therefore the lord of the vineyard do? he will come and destroy the husbandmen, and will give the vineyard unto others which shall render him the fruit in their seasons." And when they heard *it*, they said, "God forbid." And he beheld them, and said, "Have ye not read this scripture: 'The stone which the builders rejected is become the head of the corner: whosoever shall fall on this stone shall be broken: but on whomsoever it shall fall, it will grind him to powder. This was the Lord's doing, and it is marvelous in our eyes'? Therefore say I unto you, The kingdom of God shall be taken from you, and given to a nation bringing forth the fruits thereof."

PARABLE OF THE MARRIAGE FEAST

And Jesus answered and spake unto them again by parables, and said, "The kingdom of heaven is like unto a certain king, which made a marriage for his son, and sent forth his servants to call them that were bidden to the wedding: and they would not come. Again, he sent forth other servants, saying, 'Tell them which are bidden, "Behold, I have prepared my dinner: my oxen and *my* fatlings *are* killed, and all things *are* ready: come unto the marriage." ' But they made light of *it*, and went their ways, one to his farm, another to his merchandise: and the remnant took his servants, and entreated *them* spitefully, and slew *them*. But when the king heard *thereof*, he was wroth: and he sent forth his armies, and destroyed those murderers, and burned up their city. Then saith he to his servants, 'The wedding is ready, but they which were bidden were not worthy. Go ye therefore into the highways and as many as ye shall find, bid to the marriage.' So those servants went out into the highways, and gathered together all as many as they found, both bad and good: and the wedding was furnished with guests. And when the king came in to see the guests, he saw there a man which had not on a wedding garment: and he saith unto him, 'Friend, how camest thou in hither not having a wedding garment?' And he was speechless. Then said the king to the servants, 'Bind him hand and foot, and take him away and cast *him* into outer darkness; there shall be weeping and gnashing of teeth. For many are called but few *are* chosen.' "*

And when the chief priests and the scribes and Pharisees had heard his parables, they perceived that he spake against them, and they sought to lay hands on him the same hour, but they feared the people, because they took him for a prophet.

THE PHARISEES AND SADDUCEES TEST JESUS

Then went the Pharisees their way, and took counsel how they might entangle him in *his* talk. And they watched *him*, and sent forth unto him spies, certain of their disciples and of the Herodians, which should feign themselves just men, that they might take hold of his words, that so they might deliver him unto the power and authority of the governor. And when they were come, they say unto him, "Master, we know that thou art true and sayest and teachest rightly, neither carest thou for any man: for thou regardest not the person of men, but teachest the way of God in truth. Tell us therefore, what thinkest thou? Is it lawful for us to give tribute unto Caesar, or not? Shall we give, or shall we not give?" But Jesus perceived their craftiness [wickedness—Matthew], and said unto

---

*The parable of the wedding feast is very similar to p. 108, but the context and conclusion are quite different.

them, "Why tempt ye me, ye hypocrites? Shew me a penny, that I may see it." And they brought unto him a penny. And he saith unto them, "Whose image and superscription hath it?" They answered and said unto him, "Caesar's." Then Jesus saith unto them, "Render therefore unto Caesar the things which are Caesar's, and unto God the things that are God's." And they could not take hold of his words before the people: and they marvelled at his answer, and held their peace, and left him, and went their way.

The same day came to him the Sadducees, which deny that there is any resurrection, and asked him, saying, "Master, Moses wrote unto us, 'If a man die, having no children, his brother shall marry his wife, and raise up seed unto his brother.' Now there were with us seven brethren: and the first took a wife, and died without children. And the second took her to wife, and he died childless. And the third took her; and in like manner the seven had her, and they left no children, and died. And last of all the woman died also. Therefore in the resurrection, when they shall rise, whose wife shall she be of the seven? for all seven had her to wife." Jesus answered and said unto them, "Ye do err, not knowing the scriptures, nor the power of God. The children of this world marry, and are given in marriage: but they which shall be accounted worthy to obtain that world, and the resurrection from the dead, neither marry, nor are given in marriage, but are as the angels of God in heaven: neither can they die any more: for they are equal unto the angels; and are the children of God, being children of the resurrection. And as touching the resurrection of the dead, that they are raised, have ye not read that which was spoken unto you by God in the book of Moses, how in the bush God spake unto him, saying, 'I am the God of Abraham, and the God of Isaac, and the God of Jacob?' He is not the God of the dead, but the God of the living: for all do live unto him. Ye therefore do greatly err." And when the multitude heard *this*, they were astonished at his doctrine.

THE GREAT COMMANDMENT

But when the Pharisees had heard that he had put the Sadducees to silence, they were gathered together. And then one of the scribes, a lawyer, came, and having heard them reasoning together, and perceiving that he had answered them well, asked *him a question*, tempting him, and saying, "Master, which is the great commandment of all in the law?" Jesus said unto him, "The first of all the commandments *is*, 'Hear, O Israel, The Lord our God is one Lord: and thou shalt love the Lord thy God with all thy heart, and with all thy soul, and with all thy mind, and with all thy strength.' This is the first and great commandment. And the second is like unto it, 'Thou shalt love thy neighbor as thyself.' There is none other commandment greater than these. On these two commandments hang all the law and the prophets." And the scribe said unto him, "Well, Master, thou hast said the truth: for there is one God; and there is none other but he: and to love him with all the heart and with all the understanding, and with all the soul, and with all the strength, and to love *his* neighbour as himself, is more than all whole burnt offerings and sacrifices." And when Jesus saw that he answered discreetly, he said unto him, "Thou art not far from the kingdom of God."

THE NATURE OF THE CHRIST

While the Pharisees were gathered together while he taught in the temple, Jesus asked them, saying, "What think ye of Christ? whose son is he? How say the scribes that Christ is the son of David? For David himself called him Lord by the Holy Ghost in the book of Psalms, saying, 'The Lord said unto my Lord, "Sit thou on my right hand, till I make thine enemies thy footstool." ' If David therefore himself calleth him 'Lord,' how is he then his son?" And no man was able to answer him a word, neither durst any *man* from that day forth ask him any more *questions*. And the common people heard him gladly.

JESUS ATTACKS THE SCRIBES AND PHARISEES

Then in the audience of all the people he said unto his disciples, saying, "The scribes and the Pharisees sit in Moses' seat: all therefore whatsoever they bid you observe, *that* observe and do; but do not ye after their works: for they say, and do not. For they bind heavy burdens and grievous to be borne, and lay *them* on men's shoulders; but they *themselves* will not move them with one of their fingers. Beware of the scribes, which love to go in long robes, but all their works they do for to be seen of men: they make broad their phylacteries, and enlarge the borders of their garments, and love the uppermost rooms at feasts, and the chief seats in the synagogues, and greetings in the markets, and to be called of men, 'Rabbi, Rabbi.'* But be not ye called Rabbi: for one is your Master, *even* Christ; and all ye are brethren. And call no *man* your father upon the earth: for one is your Father, which is in heaven. Neither be ye called masters: for one is your Master, *even* Christ.†

But woe unto you, scribes and Pharisees, hypocrites! for ye shut up the kingdom of heaven against men: for ye neither go in *yourselves*, neither suffer ye them that are entering to go in. Woe unto you, scribes and Pharisees, hypocrites! for ye devour widows' houses, and for a pretence make long prayer: therefore ye shall receive the greater damnation. Woe unto you, scribes and Pharisees, hypocrites! for ye compass sea and land to make one proselyte, and when he is made, ye make him twofold more the child of hell than yourselves. Woe unto you, *ye* blind guides, which say, 'Whosoever shall swear by the temple, it is nothing; but whosoever shall swear by the gold of the temple, he is a

*This is the sort of criticism he would be likely to repeat from pp. 103–104.
†The sentence on Christ is repeated in Matthew this way.

debtor!' *Ye* fools and blind: for whether is greater, the gold, or the temple that sanctifieth the gold? And, 'Whosoever shall swear by the altar, it is nothing; but whosoever sweareth by the gift that is upon it, he is guilty.' *Ye* fools and blind: for whether *is* greater, the gift, or the altar that sanctifieth the gift? Whoso therefore shall swear by the altar, sweareth by it, and by all things thereon. And whoso shall swear by the temple, sweareth by it, and by him that dwelleth therein. And he that shall swear by heaven, sweareth by the throne of God, and by him that sitteth thereon. Woe unto you, scribes and Pharisees, hypocrites! for ye pay tithe of mint and anise and cummin, and rue and all manner of herbs, and have omitted the weightier *matters* of the law, judgment, mercy, faith, and the love of God: these ought ye to have done, and not to leave the other undone. *Ye* blind guides, which strain at a gnat, and swallow a camel. Woe unto you, scribes and Pharisees, hypocrites! for ye make clean the outside of the cup and of the platter, but within they are full of extortion and excess.* *Thou* blind Pharisee, cleanse first that *which is* within the cup and platter, that the outside of them may be clean also. Woe unto you, scribes and Pharisees, hypocrites! for ye are like unto whited sepulchres, which indeed appear beautiful outward, but are within full of dead *men's* bones, and of all uncleanness. Even so ye also outwardly appear righteous unto men, but within ye are full of hypocrisy and iniquity. Woe unto you, scribes and Pharisees, hypocrites! because ye build the tombs of the prophets, and garnish the sepulchres of the righteous, and say, 'If we had been in the days of our fathers, we would not have been partakers with them in the blood of the prophets.' Wherefore ye be witnesses unto yourselves, that ye are the children of them which killed the prophets, for they indeed killed them, and ye build their sepulchres. Fill ye up then the measure of your fathers. *Ye* serpents, ye generation of vipers, how can ye escape the damnation of hell? Therefore also said the wisdom of God, 'Behold, I will send unto you prophets, and apostles, and wise men, and scribes: and *some*

---

*Jesus stays close to his earlier condemnation throughout his speech, see pp. 103–104.

of them ye shall kill and crucify; and *some* of them shall ye
scourge in your synagogues, and persecute *them* from city to
city: that the righteous blood of all the prophets which was shed
upon the earth from the foundation of the world may be required of this generation; from the blood of righteous Abel unto
the blood of Zacharias son of Barachias, whom ye slew between
the temple and the altar.' Verily I say unto you, All these things
shall be required of this generation. O Jerusalem, Jerusalem,
thou that killest the prophets, and stonest them which are sent
unto thee, how often would I have gathered thy children together, even as a hen gathereth her chickens under *her* wings,
and ye would not! Behold, your house is left desolate, for I say
unto you, Ye shall not see me henceforth, till ye shall say,
'Blessed *is* he that cometh in the name of the Lord.' "

And Jesus sat over against the treasury, and beheld how the
people cast money into the treasury: and many that were rich
cast in much. And there came a certain poor widow, and she
threw in two mites, which make a farthing. And he called *unto
him* his disciples, and saith unto them, "Verily, I say unto you,
That this poor widow has cast more in, than all they which have
cast into the treasury: for all these have of their abundance cast
in unto the offerings of God: but she of her penury hath cast in
all the living that she had."

The same day there came certain of the Pharisees, saying unto
him, "Get thee out, and depart hence: for Herod will kill thee."
And he said unto them, "Go ye, and tell that fox, 'Behold, I cast
out devils, and I do cures to day and to morrow, and the third
day I shall be perfected. Nevertheless I must walk to day, and to
morrow, and the *day* following: for it cannot be that a prophet
perish out of Jerusalem.' "

THE END TIMES

And Jesus went out, and departed from the temple: and his
disciples came *to him* for to shew him the buildings of the

temple, how it was adorned with goodly stones and gifts, saying, "Master, see what manner of stones and what buildings *are here.*" And Jesus said unto them, "Seest thou all these great buildings? verily I say unto you, the days will come in the which there shall not be left one stone upon another, that shall not be thrown down." And as he sat upon the mount of Olives, over against the temple, Peter and James and John and Andrew asked him privately, saying, "Master, tell us when all these things shall come to pass [be fulfilled—Mark], and of the end of the world? what *shall be* the sign of thy coming?"

And Jesus answered and said unto them, "Take heed that no man deceive you. For many shall come in my name, saying, 'I am Christ,' and 'the time draweth near': and shall deceive many; go ye not therefore after them. And ye shall hear of wars and rumours of wars: see that ye be not troubled [terrified—Luke]: for all *these things* must come to pass, but the end is not yet. For nation shall rise against nation, and kingdom against kingdom: and there shall be famines, and pestilences, and earthquakes in divers places; and fearful sights and great signs shall there be from heaven. All these *are* the beginning of sorrows.

"Then shall they deliver you up to be afflicted, and shall kill you.* But when they shall lead *you*, and deliver you up, settle it in your hearts, not to meditate beforehand what ye shall speak: for I will give you a mouth and wisdom, which all your adversaries shall not be able to gainsay nor resist: but whatsoever shall be given you in that hour, that speak ye: for it is not ye that speak, but the Holy Ghost. And ye shall be betrayed both by parents, and brethren, and kinsfolks, and friends; and *some* of you shall they cause to be put to death. And ye shall be hated of all *men* for my name's sake. But there shall not an hair of your head perish. In your patience possess ye your souls. And then shall many be offended, and shall betray one another, and shall hate one another. And because iniquity shall abound, the love of

*The entire paragraph is similar to his charge on sending forth the disciples, perhaps occasioned by the fact that his earlier expectations did not come true, see p. 79.

many shall wax cold. But he that shall endure unto the end, the same shall be saved. And this gospel of the kingdom shall first be preached in all the world, for a witness unto all nations; and then shall the end come.

"When ye therefore shall see the abomination of desolation, spoken of by Daniel the prophet, standing where it ought not, in the holy place (whoso readeth, let him understand:) *and* Jerusalem compassed with armies, then know that the desolation thereof is nigh. Then let them which be in Judaea flee into the mountains; and let them which are in the midst of it depart out; let him which is on the housetop not go down into the house to take anything out of his house: and let him which is in the field not turn back again to take up his clothes.* For these be the days of vengeance, that all things which are written may be fulfilled. But woe unto them that are with child, and to them that give suck in those days! for there shall be great distress in the land, and wrath upon this people. But pray ye that your flight be not in the winter, neither on the sabbath day. For in those days shall be great affliction, such as was not since the beginning of the creation of the world which God created unto this time, no, nor ever shall be. And except that the Lord had shortened those days, no flesh should be saved: but for the elect's sake, whom he hath chosen, he hath shortened the days. And they shall fall by the edge of the sword, and shall be led away captive into all nations: and Jerusalem shall be trodden down of the Gentiles, until the times of the Gentiles be fulfilled. Then if any man shall say to you, 'Lo, here *is* Christ; or, lo, *he is* there; believe *him* not: for there shall arise false Christs, and false prophets, and shall shew great signs and wonders; insomuch that, if *it were* possible, they shall deceive [seduce—Mark] the very elect. But take heed: behold, I have told you before.

"Wherefore if they shall say unto you, 'Behold, he is in the desert'; go not forth: 'behold *he is* in the secret chambers'; believe *it* not. For as the lightning cometh out of the east, and

---

*For the same prophecy earlier, see p. 114.

shineth even unto the west; so shall also the coming of the Son of man be. And there shall be signs in the sun, and in the moon, and in the stars; and upon the earth distress of nations, with perplexity; the sea and the waves roaring; men's hearts failing them for fear, and looking after those things which are coming on the earth. But immediately after the tribulation of those days, the sun shall be darkened, and the moon shall not give her light, and the stars of heaven shall fall, and the powers that are in heaven shall be shaken. And then shall they see the sign of the Son of man coming in the clouds with great power and glory, and then all the tribes of the earth shall mourn. And then he shall send his angels with a great sound of a trumpet, and shall gather together his elect from the four winds, from the uttermost part of the earth, and from one end of heaven to another. And when these things begin to come to pass, then look up, and lift up your heads; for your redemption draweth nigh.

"Now learn a parable of the fig tree and all trees: When his branch is yet tender, and putteth forth leaves, ye know of your own selves that summer is nigh at hand. So likewise ye, when ye shall see all these things come to pass, know that the kingdom of God is near, *even* at the doors. Verily I say unto you, This generation shall not pass away, till all these things be fulfilled. Heaven and earth shall pass away, but my words shall not pass away. But of that day and hour knoweth no *man*, no, not the angels which are in heaven, neither the Son, but my Father only. Take heed to yourselves, lest at any time your hearts be overcharged with surfeiting, and drunkenness, and cares of this life, and so that day come upon you unawares. For as a snare shall it come on all them that dwell on the face of the whole earth. Watch ye therefore, and pray always, that ye may be accounted worthy to escape all these things that shall come to pass, and to stand before the Son of man: for ye know not what hour your Lord doth come.

PARABLES OF THE END TIMES

"But know this, that if the goodman of the house had known in what watch the thief would come, he would have watched, and would not have suffered his house to be broken up. Therefore be ye also ready: for in such an hour as ye think not the Son of man cometh." Then Peter said unto him, "Lord, speakest thou this parable unto us, or even to all?" And the Lord said, "*The Son of man is* as a man taking a far journey, who left his house, and gave authority to his servants, and to every man his work, and commanded the porter to watch. Who then is a faithful and wise servant, whom his lord hath made ruler over his household to give them their portion of meat in due season? Blessed *is* that servant, whom his lord when he cometh shall find so doing.* Verily I say unto you, That he shall make him ruler over all his goods. But and if that evil servant shall say in his heart, 'My lord delayeth his coming; and shall begin to smite the menservants and maidens, and to eat and drink and to be drunken; the lord of that servant shall come in a day when he looketh not for *him*, and in an hour that he is not aware of, and shall cut him asunder, and appoint *him* his portion with the hypocrites [unbelievers—Luke]. And that servant, which knew his lord's will, and prepared not *himself*, neither did according to his will, shall be beaten with many *stripes*. But he that knew not, and did commit things worthy of stripes, shall be beaten with few *stripes*. For unto whomsoever much is given, of him shall be much required: and to whom men have committed much, of him they will ask the more; there shall be weeping and gnashing of teeth.

THE WISE AND FOOLISH VIRGINS

"Then shall the kingdom of heaven be likened unto ten virgins, which took their lamps, and went forth to meet the bridegroom.

*See p. 105.
*See p. 105.

And five of them were wise, and five *were* foolish. They that *were* foolish took their lamps, and took no oil with them: but the wise took oil in their vessels with their lamps. While the bridegroom tarried, they all slumbered and slept. And at midnight there was a cry made, 'Behold, the bridegroom cometh; go ye out to meet him!' Then all those virgins arose, and trimmed their lamps. And the foolish said unto the wise, 'Give us of your oil; for our lamps are gone out.' But the wise answered, saying, '*Not so*; lest there be not enough for us and you: but go ye rather to them that sell, and buy for yourselves.' And while they went to buy, the bridegroom came; and they that were ready went in with him to the marriage: and the door was shut. Afterward came also the other virgins, saying, 'Lord, Lord, open to us.' But he answered and said, 'Verily I say unto you, I know you not.' Watch therefore, for ye know neither the day nor the hour wherein the Son of man cometh.

PARABLE OF THE TALENTS*

"For *the kingdom of heaven* is as a certain nobleman *who* went into a far country to receive for himself a kingdom, and to return. And he called his own [ten—Luke] servants, and delivered unto them his goods [ten pounds—Luke], and said *unto* them, 'Occupy till I come.' And unto one he gave five talents, to another two, and to another one; to every man according to his several ability; and straightway took his journey. But his citizens hated him, and sent a message after him, saying, 'We will not have this *man* to reign over us.' Then he that had received the five talents went and traded with the same, and made *them* other five talents. And likewise he that *had received* two, he also

---

*In Luke this parable is placed when Jesus is "nigh unto Jerusalem." It is not likely that he would have told it twice in so short a period of time. Luke only gives the context that his followers "thought the kingdom of God should immediately appear," but that is not the lesson of the parable.

gained other two. But he that had received one went and digged in the earth, and hid his lord's money. And it came to pass after a long time, that when the lord of those servants was returned, having received the kingdom, then he commanded these servants to be called unto him, to whom he had given the money, and reckoneth with them, that he might know how much every man had gained by trading. Then came he that had received five talents and brought other five talents, saying, 'Lord, thou deliveredst unto me five talents; behold, I have gained beside them five talents more' [thy pound hath gained ten pounds—Luke]. And his lord said unto him, 'Well done, thou good and faithful servant: because thou hast been faithful over a few things, I will make thee ruler over many things: enter into the joy of thy lord; have thou authority over ten cities.' And the second that had received two talents came and said, 'Lord, thou deliveredst unto me two talents: behold, I have gained two other talents beside them' [thy pound hath gained five pounds—Luke]. And his lord said likewise unto him, 'Well done, good and faithful servant; thou hast been faithful over a few things. I will make thee ruler over many things: enter thou into the joy of thy lord. Be thou also over five cities.' Then he which had received the one talent came and said, 'Lord, I knew thee that thou art an austere [hard—Matthew] man, reaping where thou hast not sown, and gathering where thou hast not strawed [takest up that thou layedst not down—Luke]: and I feared thee, and went and hid thy talent in the earth [which I have kept laid up in a napkin— Luke]: lo, *there* thou hast *that is* thine' [thy pound—Luke]. His lord answered and said unto him, '*Thou* wicked and slothful servant, out of thine own mouth will I judge thee. Thou knewest that I was an austere man, that I reap where I sowed not, and gather where I have not strawed [taking up that I laid not down—Luke]: thou oughtest therefore to have put my money into the bank [to the exchangers—Matthew], and then at my coming I should have received mine own with usury.' And he said unto them that stood by, 'Take therefore the talent [pound—Luke] from him, and give it unto him which hath ten talents' [pounds—Luke]. (And they said unto him, 'Lord, he hath ten pounds.') 'For I say unto you, That unto every one which hath shall be given, and he shall have more abundance; but from him that hath not shall be taken away even that which he hath. And cast ye the unprofitable servant into outer darkness. But those mine enemies, which would not that I should reign over them, bring hither, and slay them before me.' There shall be weeping and gnashing of teeth. Watch ye therefore: for ye know not when the master of the house cometh, at even, or at midnight, or at the cock crowing, or in the morning: lest coming suddenly, he find you sleeping. And what I say unto you, I say unto all, Watch.

THE JUDGMENT OF THE NATIONS

"When the Son of man shall come in his glory, and all the holy angels with him, then shall he sit upon the throne of his glory: and before him shall be gathered all nations: and he shall separate them one from another, as a shepherd divideth *his* sheep from the goats: and he shall set the sheep on his right hand, but the goats on the left. Then shall the King say unto them on his right hand, 'Come, ye blessed of my Father, inherit the kingdom prepared for you from the foundation of the world: for I was an hungred, and ye gave me meat: I was thirsty, and ye gave me drink: I was a stranger, and ye took me in: naked, and ye clothed me: I was sick, and ye visited me: I was in prison, and ye came unto me.' Then shall the righteous answer him, saying, 'Lord, when saw we thee an hungred, and fed *thee?* or thirsty, and gave *thee* drink? When saw we thee a stranger, and took *thee* in? or naked, and clothed *thee?* Or when saw we thee sick, or in prison, and came unto thee?' And the King shall answer and say unto them, 'Verily I say unto you, Inasmuch as ye have done *it* unto one of the least of these my brethren, ye have done *it* unto me.' Then shall he say also unto them on the left hand,

'Depart from me, ye cursed, into everlasting fire, prepared for the devil and his angels: for I was an hungred, and ye gave me no meat: I was thirsty, and ye gave me no drink: I was a stranger, and ye took me not in: naked, and ye clothed me not: sick, and in prison, and ye visited me not.' Then shall they also answer him, saying, 'Lord, when saw we thee an hungred, or athirst, or a stranger, or naked, or sick, or in prison, and did not minister unto thee?' Then shall he answer them, saying, 'Verily I say unto you, Inasmuch as ye did *it* not to one of the least of these, ye did *it* not to me.' And these shall go away into everlasting punishment: but the righteous into life eternal."

And in the day time he was teaching in the temple: and at night he went out, and abode in the mount that is called *the mount* of Olives. And all the people came early in the morning to him in the temple, for to hear him.

THE PASSOVER

Now the feast of unleavened bread drew nigh, which is called the Passover. And it came to pass, when Jesus had finished all these sayings, he said unto his disciples, "Ye know that after two days is the feast of the passover, and of unleavened bread, and the Son of man is betrayed to be crucified."

Then assembled together the chief priests, and the scribes, and the elders of the people, unto the palace of the high priest, who was called Caiaphas, and consulted that they might take Jesus by subtilty and kill him, for they feared the people. But they said, "Not on the feast day, lest there be an uproar among the people."

And being in Bethany in the house of Simon the leper, as he sat at meat, Mary, *the sister of Lazarus*, having an alabaster box of a pound of ointment of spikenard, very costly; and she brake the box, and poured it on his head, as he sat at meat, and anointed the feet of Jesus, and wiped his feet with her hair: and the house was filled with the odour of the ointment.* But when his disciples saw it, they had indignation within themselves, and said, "To what purpose was this waste of the ointment made?" Then saith one of his disciples, Judas Iscariot, Simon's son, which would betray him, "Why was not this ointment sold for more than three hundred pence and given to the poor?" And they murmured against her. This he said, not that he cared for the poor; but because he was a thief, and had the bag, and bare what was put therein. And Jesus said, "Let her alone; why trouble ye her? She hath wrought a good work upon me. For ye have the poor with you always, and whensoever ye will, ye may do them good; but me ye have not always. She hath done what she could. For in that she hath poured this ointment on my body, she is come aforehand to anoint my body against the day of my burying [for my burial—Matthew]. Verily I say unto you, wheresoever this gospel shall be preached throughout the whole world, this also that she hath done shall be spoken of for a memorial of her."

Then entered Satan into Judas surnamed Iscariot, being of the number of the twelve. And he went his way, and communed with the chief priests and captains, how he might betray him unto them, and said unto them, "What will ye give me, and I will deliver him unto you?" And when they heard it, they were glad. And they covenanted with him to give him thirty pieces of silver. And from that time he sought opportunity how he might conveniently betray him unto them in the absence of the multitude.

THE LAST SUPPER

Then came the first day of unleavened bread when the passover must be killed, and the disciples came to Jesus and said unto him, "Where wilt thou that we prepare for thee that thou may-

---

*There are real differences both in the event and in the lesson that Jesus draws on pp. 52–53.

est eat the passover?" Then he sent Peter and John, saying, "Go and prepare us the passover, that we may eat. Go ye into the city. Behold, when you are entered into the city, there shall a man meet you, bearing a pitcher of water: follow him into the house where he entereth in, and say ye to the goodman of the house, 'The Master saith unto thee, my time is at hand; I will keep the passover at thy house. Where is the guestchamber, where I shall eat the passover with my disciples?' And he will shew you a large upper room furnished and prepared: there make ready for us." And his disciples went forth as Jesus had appointed them, and came into the city, and found as he had said unto them: and they made ready the passover.

And in the evening, when the hour was come, he cometh and sat down with the twelve apostles with him. When Jesus knew that his hour was come that he should depart out of this world unto the Father, having loved his own which were in the world, he loved them unto the end. And he said unto them, "With desire I have desired to eat this passover with you before I suffer; for I say unto you, I will not any more eat thereof, until it be fulfilled in the kingdom of God."

And supper being ended,* the devil having now put into the heart of Judas Iscariot, Simon's son, to betray him; Jesus knowing that the Father had given all things into his hands, and that he was come from God, and went to God; he riseth from supper, and laid aside his garments; and took a towel and girded himself. After that he poureth water into a bason, and began to wash the disciples' feet, and to wipe *them* with the towel wherewith he was girded. Then cometh he to Simon Peter: and Peter saith unto him, "Lord, dost thou wash my feet?" Jesus answered and said unto him, "What I do thou knowest not now; but thou shalt know hereafter." Peter saith unto him, "Thou shalt never wash my feet." Jesus answered him, "If I wash thee not, thou hast no part with me." Simon Peter saith unto him, "Lord, not

---

*Some gospels have the bread "as they were eating," but the cup is always after supper. It is perhaps helpful to think of a long and congenial supper with conversation throughout.

my feet only, but also *my* hands and *my* head." Jesus saith to him, "He that is washed needeth not save to wash *his* feet, but is clean every whit: and ye are clean, but not all." For he knew who should betray him; therefore said he, "Ye are not all clean." So after he had washed their feet, and had taken his garments, and was set down again, he said unto them, "Know ye what I have done to you? Ye call me Master and Lord: and ye say well; for *so* I am. If I then, *your* Lord and Master, have washed your feet; ye also ought to wash one another's feet. For I have given you an example, that ye should do as I have done to you. Verily, verily, I say unto you, The servant is not greater than his lord; neither he that is sent greater than he that sent him. If ye know these things, happy are ye if ye do them. I speak not of you all: I know whom I have chosen: but that the scripture may be fulfilled, 'He that eateth bread with me hath lifted up his heel against me.' Now I tell you before it come, that, when it is come to pass, ye may believe that I am *he*. Verily, verily, I say unto you, He that receiveth whomsoever I send receiveth me; and he that receiveth me receiveth him that sent me."

THE EUCHARIST

And he took bread, and gave thanks and blessed and brake it, and gave it to the disciples, and said, "This is my body which is given for you. Take, eat; this do in remembrance of me." Likewise also he took the cup [after supper—Luke], and when he had given thanks, he gave it to them, saying, "This cup is the new testament in my blood, which is shed for you and for many for the remission of sins. Take this, and divide it among yourselves. Drink, ye all, of it. Verily I say unto you, I will not henceforth drink of this fruit of the vine until the kingdom of God shall come; until that day when I drink it new with you in God my Father's kingdom."

When Jesus had thus said, he was troubled in spirit, and testified, and said, [And as they sat and did eat—Luke] "Verily, verily,

I say unto you, that one of you which eateth with me shall betray me. Behold the hand of him that betrayeth me is with me on the table. The Son of man indeed goeth, as it is written of him [was determined—Luke]: but woe to that man by whom the Son of man is betrayed! good were it for that man if he had never been born." Then the disciples looked one on another, doubting of whom he spake. And they began to enquire among themselves, which of them it was that should do this thing. And they began to be exceeding sorrowful, and began every one of them to say unto him one by one, "Lord, is it I?" and another said, "Is it I?" And he answered and said, "It is one of the twelve that dippeth his hand with me in the dish, the same shall betray me." Then Judas, which betrayed him, answered and said, "Master, is it I?" He said unto him, "Thou hast said."

Now there was leaning on Jesus' bosom one of his disciples, whom Jesus loved. Simon Peter therefore beckoned to him, that he should ask who it should be of whom he spake. He then lying on Jesus' breast saith unto him, "Lord, who is it?" Jesus answered, "He it is, to whom I shall give a sop, when I have dipped *it*." And when he had dipped the sop, he gave *it* to Judas Iscariot, *the son* of Simon. And after the sop Satan entered into him. Then said Jesus unto him, "That thou doest, do quickly." Now no man at the table knew for what intent he spake this unto him. For some *of them* thought, because Judas had the bag, that Jesus had said unto him, "Buy *those things* that we have need of against the feast"; or, that he should give something to the poor. He then having received the sop went immediately out: and it was night.

And Jesus saith unto them, "All ye shall be offended because of me this night: for it is written, 'I will smite the shepherd, and the sheep of the flock shall be scattered abroad.' But after that I am risen again, I will go before you into Galilee." But Peter said unto him, "Although all men shall be offended because of thee, yet will I never be offended." And the Lord said, "Simon, Simon, behold Satan hath desired to have you, that he may sift you as wheat: but I have prayed for thee, that thy faith fail not: and when thou art converted, strengthen thy brethren."

JESUS PROPHESIES PETER'S DENIAL

Jesus said, "Now is the Son of man glorified, and God is glorified in him. If God be glorified in him, God shall also glorify him in himself, and shall straightway glorify him. Little children, yet a little while I am with you. Ye shall seek me: and as I said unto the Jews,* whither I go, ye cannot come: so now I say to you. A new commandment I give unto you, That ye love one another: as I have loved you, that ye also love one another. By this shall all men know that ye are my disciples, if ye have love one to another." Simon Peter said unto him, "Lord, whither goest thou?" Jesus answered him, "Whither I go, thou canst not follow me now: but thou shalt follow me afterwards." Peter said unto him, "Lord, why cannot I follow thee now? I am ready to go with thee both into prison, and to death. I will lay down my life for thy sake." Jesus answered him, "Wilt thou lay down thy life for my sake? Verily I say unto thee, that this day, even in this night before the cock crow [twice—Mark], thou shalt thrice deny that thou knowest me." But he spake the more vehemently, "Though I should die with thee, yet will I not deny thee in any wise." Likewise also said all the disciples.

"I AM THE WAY, THE TRUTH, AND THE LIFE"

"Let not your heart be troubled: ye believe in God, believe also in me. In my Father's house are many mansions: if *it were* not *so*, I would have told you. I go to prepare a place for you. And if I go and prepare a place for you, I will come again, and receive you unto myself; that where I am, *there* ye may be also. And whither I go ye know, and the way ye know." Thomas saith unto him, "Lord, we know not whither thou goest; and how can we know the way?" Jesus saith unto him, "I am the way, the truth, and the life: no man cometh unto the Father, but by me. If ye had

*See p. 58.

known me, ye should have known my Father also: and from henceforth ye know him, and have seen him." Philip saith unto him, "Lord, shew us the Father, and it sufficeth us." Jesus saith unto him, "Have I been so long time with you, and yet hast thou not known me, Philip? he that hath seen me hath seen the Father; and how sayest thou *then*, 'Shew us the Father'? Believest thou not that I am in the Father, and the Father in me? the words that I speak unto you I speak not of myself: but the Father that dwelleth in me, he doeth the works. Believe me that I *am* in the Father, and the Father in me: or else believe me for the very works' sake. Verily, verily, I say unto you, He that believeth on me, the works that I do shall he do also; and greater *works* than these shall he do; because I go unto my Father. And whatsoever ye shall ask in my name, that will I do, that the Father may be glorified in the Son. If ye shall ask any thing in my name, I will do *it*.

THE PROMISE OF THE SPIRIT

"If ye love me, keep my commandments. And I will pray the Father, and he shall give you another Comforter, that he may abide with you for ever; *even* the Spirit of truth; whom the world cannot receive, because it seeth him not, neither knoweth him: but ye know him; for he dwelleth with you, and shall be in you. I will not leave you comfortless: I will come to you. Yet a little while, and the world seeth me no more; but ye see me: because I live, ye shall live also. At that day ye shall know that I *am* in my Father, and ye in me, and I in you. He that hath my commandments, and keepeth them, he it is that loveth me: and he that loveth me shall be loved of my Father, and I will love him, and will manifest myself to him." Judas saith unto him, not Iscariot, "Lord, how is it that thou wilt manifest thyself unto us, and not unto the world?" Jesus answered and said unto him, "If a man love me, he will keep my words: and my Father will love him, and we will come unto him, and make our abode with him. He that loveth me not keepeth not my sayings: and the word which ye hear is not mine, but the Father's which sent me. These things have I spoken unto you, being *yet* present with you. But the Comforter, *which is* the Holy Ghost, whom the Father will send in my name, he shall teach you all things, and bring all things to your remembrance, whatsoever I have said unto you. Peace I leave with you, my peace I give unto you: not as the world giveth, give I unto you. Let not your heart be troubled, neither let it be afraid. Ye have heard how I said unto you, I go away, and come *again* unto you. If ye loved me, ye would rejoice, because I said, I go unto the Father: for my Father is greater than I. And now I have told you before it come to pass, that, when it is come to pass, ye might believe. Hereafter I will not talk much with you: for the prince of this world cometh, and hath nothing in me. But that the world may know that I love the Father; and as the Father gave me commandment, even so I do. Arise, let us go hence.*

THE TRUE VINE

"I am the true vine, and my Father is the husbandman. Every branch in me that beareth not fruit he taketh away: and every *branch* that beareth fruit, he purgeth it, that it may bring forth more fruit. Now ye are clean through the word which I have spoken unto you. Abide in me, and I in you. As the branch cannot bear fruit of itself, except it abide in the vine; no more can ye, except ye abide in me. I am the vine, ye *are* the branches: He that abideth in me, and I in him, the same bringeth forth much fruit: for without me ye can do nothing. If a man abide not in me, he is cast forth as a branch, and is withered; and men gather them, and cast *them* into the fire, and

---

*Jesus seems to have had a second thought and continued his talk (all in John).

they are burned. If ye abide in me, and my words abide in you, ye shall ask what ye will, and it shall be done unto you. Herein is my Father glorified, that ye bear much fruit; so shall ye be my disciples. As the Father hath loved me, so have I loved you: continue ye in my love.

GREATER LOVE HAS NO MAN

If ye keep my commandments, ye shall abide in my love; even as I have kept my Father's commandments, and abide in his love. These things have I spoken unto you, that my joy might remain in you, and *that* your joy might be full. This is my commandment, That ye love one another, as I have loved you. Greater love hath no man than this, that a man lay down his life for his friends. Ye are my friends, if ye do whatsoever I command you. Henceforth I call you not servants; for the servant knoweth not what his lord doeth: but I have called you friends; for all things that I have heard of my Father I have made known unto you. Ye have not chosen me, but I have chosen you, and ordained you, that ye should go and bring forth fruit, and *that* your fruit should remain: that whatsoever ye shall ask of the Father in my name, he may give it you. These things I command you, that ye love one another. If the world hate you, ye know that it hated me before *it hated* you.

"If ye were of the world, the world would love his own: but because ye are not of the world, but I have chosen you out of the world, therefore the world hateth you. Remember the word that I said unto you, 'The servant is not greater than his lord.' If they have persecuted me, they will also persecute you; if they have kept my saying, they will keep your's also. But all these things will they do unto you for my name's sake, because they know not him that sent me. If I had not come and spoken unto them, they had not had sin: but now they have no cloke for their sin. He that hateth me hateth my Father also. If I had not done among them the works which none other man did, they had not had sin: but now have they both seen and hated both me and my Father. But *this cometh to pass*, that the word might be fulfilled that is written in their law, 'They hated me without a cause.' But when the Comforter is come, whom I will send unto you from the Father, *even* the Spirit of truth, which proceedeth from the Father, he shall testify of me: and ye also shall bear witness, because ye have been with me from the beginning.

"These things have I spoken unto you, that ye should not be offended. They shall put you out of the synagogues: yea, the time cometh, that whosoever killeth you will think that he doeth God service. And these things will they do unto you, because they have not known the Father, nor me. But these things have I told you, that when the time shall come, ye may remember that I told you of them. And these things I said not unto you at the beginning, because I was with you. But now I go my way to him that sent me; and none of you asketh me, 'Whither goest thou?' But because I have said these things unto you, sorrow hath filled your heart. Nevertheless I tell you the truth; It is expedient for you that I go away: for if I go not away, the Comforter will not come unto you; but if I depart, I will send him unto you. And when he is come, he will reprove the world of sin, and of righteousness, and of judgment: of sin, because they believe not on me; of righteousness, because I go to my Father, and ye see me no more; of judgment, because the prince of this world is judged. I have yet many things to say unto you, but ye cannot bear them now. Howbeit when he, the Spirit of truth, is come, he will guide you into all truth: for he shall not speak of himself; but whatsoever he shall hear, *that* shall he speak: and he will shew you things to come. He shall glorify me: for he shall receive of mine, and shall shew *it* unto you. All things that the Father hath are mine: therefore said I, that he shall take of mine, and shall shew it unto you. A little while, and ye shall not see me: and again, a little while, and ye shall see me, because I go to the Father."

Then said *some* of his disciples among themselves, "What is this that he saith unto us, 'A little while, and ye shall not see me: and again, a little while, and ye shall see me': and 'Because I go to the Father'?" They said therefore, "What is this that he saith, 'A little while'? we cannot tell what he saith."

PROMISE OF ANSWERED PRAYER

Now Jesus knew that they were desirous to ask him, and said unto them, "Do ye enquire among yourselves of that I said, "A little while, and ye shall not see me: and again, a little while, and ye shall see me'? Verily, verily, I say unto you, That ye shall weep and lament, but the world shall rejoice: and ye shall be sorrowful, but your sorrow shall be turned into joy. A woman when she is in travail hath sorrow, because her hour is come: but as soon as she is delivered of the child, she remembereth no more the anguish, for joy that a man is born into the world. And ye now therefore have sorrow: but I will see you again, and your heart shall rejoice, and your joy no man taketh from you. And in that day ye shall ask me nothing. Verily, verily, I say unto you, Whatsoever ye shall ask the Father in my name, he will give *it* you. Hitherto have ye asked nothing in my name: ask, and ye shall receive, that your joy may be full. These things have I spoken unto you in proverbs: but the time cometh, when I shall no more speak unto you in proverbs, but I shall shew you plainly of the Father. At that day ye shall ask in my name: and I say not unto you, that I will pray the Father for you: for the Father himself loveth you, because ye have loved me, and have believed that I came out from God. I came forth from the Father, and am come into the world: again, I leave the world, and go to the Father." His disciples said unto him, "Lo, now speakest thou plainly, and speakest no proverb. Now are we sure that thou knowest all things, and needest not that any man should ask thee: by this we believe that thou camest forth from God." Jesus answered them, "Do ye now believe? Behold, the hour cometh, yea, is now come, that ye shall be scattered, every man to his own, and shall leave me alone: and yet I am not alone, because the Father is with me. These things I have spoken unto you, that in me ye might have peace. In the world ye shall have tribulation: but be of good cheer; I have overcome the world."

CHRIST'S PRAYER OF UNITY

These words spake Jesus, and lifted up his eyes to heaven, and said, "Father, the hour is come; glorify thy Son, that thy Son also may glorify thee: as thou hast given him power over all flesh, that he should give eternal life to as many as thou hast given him. And this is life eternal, that they might know thee the only true God, and Jesus Christ, whom thou hast sent. I have glorified thee on the earth: I have finished the work which thou gavest me to do. And now, O Father, glorify thou me with thine own self with the glory which I had with thee before the world was. I have manifested thy name unto the men which thou gavest me out of the world: thine they were, and thou gavest them me; and they have kept thy word. Now they have known that all things whatsoever thou hast given me are of thee. For I have given unto them the words which thou gavest me; and they have received *them*, and have known surely that I came out from thee, and they have believed that thou didst send me. I pray for them: I pray not for the world, but for them which thou hast given me; for they are thine. And all mine are thine, and thine are mine; and I am glorified in them. And now I am no more in the world, but these are in the world, and I come to thee. Holy Father, keep through thine own name those whom thou hast given me, that they may be one, as we *are*. While I was with them in the world, I kept them in thy name: those that thou gavest me I have kept, and none of them is lost, but the son of perdition; that the scripture might be fulfilled. And now come I to thee; and these things I speak in the world, that they might have my joy fulfilled in themselves. I have given them thy word; and the world hath hated them, because they are not of the world, even as I am not of the world. I pray not that thou shouldest take them out of the world, but that thou shouldest keep them from the evil. They are not of the world, even as I am not of the world. Sanctify them through thy truth: thy word is truth. As thou hast sent me into the world, even so have I also sent them into the world. And for their sakes I sanctify myself, that they also might be sanctified through the truth. Neither pray I for these alone, but for them also which shall believe on me through their word; that they all may be one; as thou, Father, *art* in me, and I in thee, that they also may be one in us: that the world may believe that thou hast sent me. And the glory which thou gavest me I have given them; that they may be one, even as we are one: I in them, and thou in me, that they may be made perfect in one; and that the world may know that thou hast sent me, and hast loved them, as thou hast loved me. Father, I will that they also, whom thou hast given me, be with me where I am; that they may behold my glory, which thou hast given me: for thou lovedst me before the foundation of the world. O righteous Father, the world hath not known thee: but I have known thee, and these have known that thou hast sent me. And I have declared unto them thy name, and will declare *it:* that the love wherewith thou hast loved me may be in them, and I in them."

And he said unto them, "When I sent you without purse, and scrip, and shoes, lacked ye any thing?" And they said, "Nothing." Then said he unto them, "But now, he that hath a purse, let him take *it,* and likewise *his* scrip: and he that hath no sword, let him sell his garment, and buy one. For I say unto you, that this that is written must yet be accomplished in me, 'And he was reckoned among the transgressors': for the things concerning me have an end." And they said, "Lord, behold, here *are* two swords." And he said unto them, "It is enough."

GETHSEMANE

And when they had sung a hymn, they went out, as he was wont, to the mount of Olives: and his disciples also followed him; over the brook Cedron, where was a garden called Gethsemane, into the which he entered, and his disciples followed him. And he saith to his disciples, "Sit ye here, while I go and pray yonder. Pray that ye enter not into temptation." And he took with him Peter, and James and John, the two sons of Zebedee and began to be sorrowful and very heavy. Then saith he unto them, "My soul is exceeding sorrowful, even unto death; tarry here and watch with me." And he went a little farther forward and was withdrawn from them about a stone's cast, and kneeled down, and fell on his face on the ground, and prayed that, if it were possible, the hour might pass from him. And he said, "Abba, Father, all things are possible unto thee: if thou be willing [if it be possible—Matthew], take away this cup [let this cup pass—Matthew] from me: nevertheless not what I will, but what thou wilt [not my will, but thine—Luke] be done." And there appeared an angel unto him from heaven, strengthening him. And being in an agony he prayed more earnestly; and his sweat was as it were great drops of blood falling down to the ground. And when he rose up from prayer, he cometh unto the disciples and findeth them sleeping for sorrow, and saith unto Peter, "What, sleepest thou, could ye not watch with me one hour? Watch and pray, lest ye enter not into temptation: the spirit indeed is willing, but the flesh is weak." He went away again the second time, and prayed, saying, "O my Father, if this cup may not pass away from me, except I drink it, thy will be done." And he came and found them asleep again: for their eyes were heavy neither wist they what to answer him. And he left them, and went away again, and prayed the third time, saying the same words. Then cometh he to his disciples, and saith unto them, "Sleep on now, and take *your* rest: it is enough; behold, the hour is at hand. Behold, the Son of man is betrayed into the hands of sinners. Rise, let us be going; behold, he is at hand that doth betray me."

THE BETRAYAL

And Judas also, which betrayed him, knew the place: for Jesus ofttimes resorted thither with his disciples. And immediately, while he yet spake, Judas, one of the twelve, having received a band of *men* and officers from the chief priests and Pharisees and the scribes and the elders, cometh thither with a great multitude with lanterns and torches and swords and staves. And he that betrayed him had given them a token, saying, "Whomsoever I shall kiss, that same is he: take him, and lead *him* away safely." And as soon as he was come, he goeth straightway to him, and saith, "Master, master"; and kissed him. And Jesus said unto him, "Friend, wherefore art thou come? Judas, betrayest thou the Son of man with a kiss?"

Jesus therefore, knowing all things that should come upon him, went forth, and said unto them, "Whom seek ye?" They answered him, "Jesus of Nazareth." Jesus saith unto them, "I am *he.*" And Judas also, which betrayed him, stood with them. As soon as he had said unto them, "I am *he,*" they went backward, and fell to the ground. Then asked he them again, "Whom seek ye?" And they said, "Jesus of Nazareth." Jesus answered, "I have told you that I am he: if therefore ye seek me, let these go their way"; that the saying might be fulfilled, which he spake, "Of them which thou gavest me have I lost none." And they laid their hands on him, and took him.

When they which were about him saw what would follow, they said unto him, "Lord, shall we smite with the sword?" Then Simon Peter having a sword drew it, and smote the high priest's servant, and cut off his right ear. The servant's name was Malchus. Then said Jesus unto Peter, "Put up thy sword into the sheath: for all they that take the sword shall perish with the sword. The cup which my Father hath given me, shall I not drink it? Suffer ye thus far." And he touched his ear and healed him. "Thinkest thou that I cannot now pray to my Father, and he shall presently give more than twelve legions of angels? But how then shall the scriptures be fulfilled, that thus it must be?"

Then Jesus said unto the chief priests, and captains of the temple, and the elders, which were come to him, "Be ye come out, as against a thief, with swords and staves to take me? When I was daily with you in the temple teaching, ye stretched forth no hands against me: but this is your hour, and the power of darkness." But all this was done, that the scriptures of the prophets might be fulfilled. Then all the disciples forsook him, and fled. And there followed him a certain young man, having a linen cloth cast about *his* naked *body*; and the young men laid hold on him: and he left the linen cloth, and fled from them naked.

Then the band and the captains and officers of the Jews took Jesus, and bound him. And led him away to Annas first; for he was father in law to Caiaphas, which was the high priest that same year. Now Caiaphas was he, which gave counsel to the Jews, that it was expedient that one man should die for the people. Now Annas had sent him bound unto Caiaphas. And they that had laid hold on Jesus led him away to Caiaphas the high priest, where the scribes and the elders were assembled. But Simon Peter followed him afar off unto the high priest's palace, and went in, and when they had kindled a fire in the midst of the hall, and were set down together, he sat with the servants, to see the end, and so did another disciple; that disciple was known unto the high priest, and went in with Jesus into the palace of the high priest.

PETER'S DENIAL

But Peter stood at the door without. Then went out that other disciple, which was known unto the high priest, and spake unto her that kept the door, and brought in Peter. And the servants and officers stood there, who had made a fire of coals; for it was cold: and they warmed themselves: and Peter stood with them, and warmed himself at the fire. Then the damsel that kept the door, one of the maids of the high priest, beheld him as he sat by the fire, and earnestly looked upon him, and said, "This man was also with Jesus of Nazareth [Galilee—Matthew]. Art not thou also one of his disciples?" And he denied him before them all, saying, "Woman, I am not. I know him not, neither understand I what thou sayest." And he went out into the porch [and the cock crew—Mark]. And when he was gone out into the porch, another maid saw him, and began to say to them that stood by, "This fellow was also one of them with Jesus of Nazareth." And again he denied it, with an oath, "I am not. I do not know the man." And about the space of one hour after, one of the servants of the high priest, being his kinsman whose ear Peter cut off, came unto him and confidently affirmed, saying, "Of a truth this fellow also was with him: for he is a Galilean. Surely thou also art one of them; for thy speech bewrayeth thee. Did not I see thee in the garden with him?" And Peter said, "Man, I know not what thou sayest." Then began he to curse and to swear, saying, "I know not this man of whom ye speak." And immediately, while he yet spake, the cock crew [a second time—Mark]. And the Lord turned and looked upon Peter. And Peter remembered the word of the Lord, how he had said unto him, "Before the cock crow [twice—Mark], thou shalt deny me thrice." And when he thought thereon, he went out and wept bitterly.

CHRIST BEFORE CAIAPHAS

The high priest then asked Jesus of his disciples, and of his doctrine. Jesus answered him, "I spake openly to the world; I ever taught in the synagogue, and in the temple, whither the Jews always resort; and in secret have I said nothing. Why askest thou me? ask them which heard me, what I have said unto them; behold, they know what I said." And when he had thus spoken, one of the officers which stood by struck Jesus with the palm of his hand, saying, "Answerest thou the high priest so?" Jesus answered him, "If I have spoken evil, bear witness of the evil: but if well, why smitest thou me?" Now the chief priests, and elders, and all the council, sought false witness against Jesus, to put him to death; but found none; yea, though many false witnesses came, yet their witness agreed not together. At the last came two false witnesses, and said, "We heard this *fellow* say, 'I am able to destroy the temple of God that is made with hands, and to build another made without hands in three days.' " But neither so did their witness agree together. And the high priest arose, and said unto him, "Answerest thou nothing? what *is it which* these witness against thee?" But Jesus held his peace and answered nothing. And the high priest answered and said unto him, "I adjure thee by the living God, that thou tell us whether thou be the Christ, the Son of God" [the Blessed—Mark]. And he said unto them, "If I tell you, ye will not believe; and if I also ask *you*, ye will not answer me, nor let *me* go." Then said they all, "Art thou then the Son of God?" And he said unto them, "Thou hast said: I am; nevertheless I say unto you, Hereafter shall ye see the Son of man sitting on the right hand of the power of God, and coming in the clouds of heaven." Then the high priest rent his clothes, saying, "He hath spoken blasphemy; what further need have we of witnesses? Behold, now ye have heard his blasphemy of his own mouth. What think ye?" They all condemned him and said, "He is guilty of death." Then did they spit in his face, and blindfolded him [covered his face—Mark], and buffeted him; and others smote *him* with the palms of their hands, saying, "Prophesy unto us, thou Christ. Who is he that smote thee?" And many other things blasphemously spake they against him.

JUDAS'S DEATH

When the morning was come, the chief priests held a consultation with the elders and scribes and the whole council against Jesus to put him to death. And when they had bound him, they led him away, and delivered him to Pontius Pilate the governor.

Then Judas, which had betrayed him, when he saw that he was condemned, repented himself, and brought again the thirty pieces of silver to the chief priests and elders, saying, "I have sinned in that I have betrayed the innocent blood." And they said, "what *is that* to us? see thou *to that*." And he cast down the pieces of silver in the temple, and departed, and went and hanged himself. And the chief priests took the silver pieces, and said, "It is not lawful for to put them into the treasury, because it is the price of blood." And they took counsel, and bought with them the potter's field, to bury strangers in. Wherefore that field was called, "The field of blood," unto this day. Then was fulfilled that which was spoken by Jeremy the prophet, saying, "And they took the thirty pieces of silver, the price of him that was valued, whom they of the children of Israel did value; and gave them for the potter's field, as the Lord appointed me."

CHRIST BEFORE PILATE

Then led they Jesus from Caiaphas unto the hall of judgment: and it was early; and they themselves went not into the judgment hall, lest they should be defiled; but that they might eat the passover. Pilate then went out unto them, and said, "What accusation bring ye against this man?" They answered and said unto him, "If he were not a malefactor, we would not have delivered him up unto thee." Then said Pilate unto them, "Take ye him, and judge him according to your law." The Jews therefore said unto him, "It is not lawful for us to put any man to death": that the saying of Jesus might be fulfilled, which he spake, signifying what death he should die. And they began to accuse him, saying, "We found this fellow perverting the nation, and forbidding to give tribute to Caesar, saying that he himself is Christ a King." Then Pilate entered into the judgment hall again, and called Jesus. And Jesus stood before the governor: and when he was accused of the chief priests and elders, he answered nothing. Then Pilate said unto him, "Hearest thou not how many things they witness against thee? answerest thou nothing?" And he answered to never a word; insomuch that the governor marvelled greatly.

And Pilate asked him, saying, "Art thou the King of the Jews?" And he answered him and said, "Thou sayest it. Sayest thou this thing of thyself, or did others tell it thee of me?" Pilate answered, "Am I a Jew? Thine own nation and the chief priests have delivered thee unto me: what hast thou done?" Jesus answered, "My kingdom is not of this world: if my kingdom were of this world, then would my servants fight, that I should not be delivered to the Jews; but now is my kingdom not from hence." Pilate therefore said unto him, "Art thou a king then?" Jesus answered, "Thou sayest that I am a king. To this end was I born, and for this cause came I into the world, that I should bear witness unto the truth. Every one that is of the truth heareth my voice." Pilate saith unto him, "What is truth?" And when he had said this, he went out again unto the Jews, and saith unto them, "I find in him no fault *at all.*"

CHRIST BEFORE HEROD

And they were the more fierce, saying, "He stirreth up the people, teaching throughout all Jewry, beginning from Galilee to this place." When Pilate heard of Galilee, he asked whether the man were a Galilaean. And as soon as he knew that he belonged unto Herod's jurisdiction he sent him to Herod, who himself also was at Jerusalem at that time.

And when Herod saw Jesus, he was exceeding glad: for he was desirous to see him of a long *season*, because he had heard many things of him; and he hoped to have seen some miracle done by him. Then he questioned with him in many words; but he answered him nothing. And the chief priests and scribes stood and vehemently accused him. And Herod with his men of war set him at nought, and mocked *him*, and arrayed him in a gorgeous robe, and sent him again to Pilate. And the same day Pilate and Herod were made friends together: for before they were at enmity between themselves.

SCOURGING AND JUDGMENT

Now at that feast the governor was wont to release unto the people a prisoner, whomsoever they desired. And Pilate, when he had called together the chief priests and the rulers and the people, said unto them, "Ye have brought this man unto me, as one that perverteth the people: and, behold, I having examined *him* before you, have found no fault in this man touching those things whereof ye accuse him: no, nor yet Herod: for I sent you to him; and, lo, nothing worthy of death is done unto him. I will therefore chastise him, and release *him*." And they had then a notable prisoner named Barabbas, which lay bound with them that had made insurrection with him, who had committed murder in the insurrection. And the multitude crying aloud began to desire him to do as he had ever done unto them. Pilate said, "Ye have a custom, that I should release unto you one at the passover: will ye therefore that I release unto you Jesus which is called Christ, the King of the Jews?" For he knew that the chief priests had delivered him for envy.

When he was set down on the judgment seat, his wife sent unto him, saying, "Have thou nothing to do with that just man: for I have suffered many things this night in a dream because of him."

But the chief priests and elders persuaded the multitude that they should ask that he should rather release Barabbas unto them and destroy Jesus. And the governor said unto them, "Whether of the twain will ye that I release unto you?" And they cried out all at once, saying, "Not this man. Away with this man, and release unto us Barabbas." Now Barabbas was a robber. Pilate therefore, willing to release Jesus, spake again to them, "What shall I do then with Jesus which is called Christ, whom ye call the King of the Jews?" They all say unto him, "Let him be crucified. Crucify him, crucify him." And the third time he said unto them, "Why, what evil hath he done? I have found no cause of death in him: I will therefore chastise him, and let him go."

Then Pilate therefore took Jesus, and scourged him. Then the soldiers of the governor led him away into the common hall, called Praetorium: and they call together the whole band *of soldiers*. And they stripped him, and clothed him with a purple [scarlet—Matthew] robe. And when they had platted a crown of thorns, they put it upon his head, and a reed in his right hand: and they bowed the knee before him, and mocked him and began to salute him, and said, "Hail, King of the Jews!" and they smote him with their hands. And they smote him on the head with the reed, and did spit upon him, and bowing their knees, worshipped him. And after that they had mocked him, they took off the purple from him, and put his own clothes on him.

Pilate therefore went forth again, and saith unto them, "Behold I bring him forth to you, that ye may know that I find no fault in him." Then came Jesus forth, wearing the crown of thorns [and the purple robe—John]. And Pilate saith unto them, "Behold the man!" When the chief priests therefore and officers saw him, they cried out, saying, "Crucify him, crucify him." Pilate saith unto them, "Take ye him, and crucify him: for I find no fault in him." The Jews answered him, "We have a law, and by our law he ought to die, because he made himself the Son of God."

When Pilate therefore heard that saying, he was the more afraid; and went again into the judgment hall, and saith unto Jesus, "Whence art thou?" But Jesus gave him no answer. Then saith Pilate unto him, "Speakest thou not unto me? knowest thou not that I have power to crucify thee, and have power to release thee?" Jesus answered, "Thou couldest have no power *at all* against me, except it were given thee from above: therefore he that delivered me unto thee hath the greater sin." And from thenceforth Pilate sought to release him: but the Jews cried out, saying, "If thou let this man go, thou art not Caesar's friend: whosoever maketh himself a king speaketh against Caesar."

When Pilate therefore heard that saying, he brought Jesus forth, and sat down in the judgment seat in a place that is called the Pavement, but in the Hebrew, Gabbatha. And it was the preparation of the passover, and about the sixth hour: and he saith unto the Jews, "Behold your King!" And they cried out the more exceedingly, "Crucify him. Away with him, away with him, crucify him." And the voices of them and of the chief priests prevailed. Pilate saith unto them, "Shall I crucify your King?" The chief priests answered, "We have no king but Caesar." When Pilate saw that he could prevail nothing, but that rather a tumult was made, he took water, and washed his hands before the multitude, saying, "I am innocent of the blood of this just person: see ye to it." Then answered all the people, and said, "His blood be on us, and on our children." And Pilate gave sentence that it should be as they required. And he released unto them him that for sedition and murder was cast into prison, whom they desired, and scourged and delivered Jesus to their will to be crucified. And they took Jesus, and led him away.

THE CRUCIFIXION

And he bearing his cross went forth, and as they came out, they laid hold upon one Simon a Cyrenian, who passed by, coming out of the country, the father of Alexander and Rufus, and on him they laid the cross, that he might bear it after Jesus. And there followed him a great company of people, and of women, which also bewailed and lamented him. But Jesus turning unto them said, "Daughters of Jerusalem, weep not for me, but weep for yourselves, and for your children. For, behold the days are coming, in the which they shall say, 'Blessed *are* the barren, and the wombs that never bare, and the paps which never gave suck.' Then shall they begin to say to the mountains, 'Fall on us'; and to the hills, 'Cover us. For if they do these things in a green tree, what shall be done in the dry?' " And there were also two other, thieves, led with him to be put to death. And when they were come to the place, which is called Calvary and in the Hebrew Golgotha, that is to say, the place of a skull, there they crucified him, and the two malefactors, one on the right hand, and the other on the left, and Jesus in the midst. And the scripture was fulfilled, which saith, "And he was numbered with the transgressors."

Then said Jesus, "Father, forgive them, for they know not what they do." And the soldiers also mocked him, and they gave him vinegar wine to drink mingled with myrrh [gall—Matthew]: and when he had tasted thereof, he would not drink. And it was third hour,* and they crucified him.

Then the soldiers, when they had crucified Jesus, took his garments, and made four parts, to every soldier a part; and also his coat: now the coat was without seam, woven from the top throughout. They said therefore among themselves, "Let us not rend it, but cast lots for it, whose it shall be": that the scripture might be fulfilled, which saith, [was spoken by the prophet— Matthew] "They parted my raiment among them, and for my vesture they did cast lots." These things therefore the soldiers did. And sitting down they watched him there.

And Pilate wrote a title, and put it on the cross. And the writing was, JESUS OF NAZARETH THE KING OF THE JEWS. This title then read many of the Jews: for the place where Jesus was crucified was nigh to the city; and it was written in Hebrew, and Greek, and Latin. Then said the chief priests of the Jews to Pilate, "Write not, 'The King of the Jews'; but 'that he said, I am King of the Jews.' " Pilate answered, "What I have written I have written."

---

*Only Mark has this strange time designation; the correct meaning would seem to be "after." All other accounts locate the time on the cross between the sixth and ninth hours.

And the people stood by beholding. And they that passed by reviled him and railed on him, wagging their heads and saying, "Thou that destroyest the temple, and buildest it in three days, save thyself. If thou be the Son of God, the king of the Jews, come down from the cross." Likewise also the chief priests with them derided him and mocking said among themselves with the scribes and elders, "He saved others; himself he cannot save. If he be Christ, the chosen of God, the King of Israel, let him now come down from the cross that we may see, and we will believe him. He trusted in God; let him deliver him now, if he will have him: for he said, 'I am the Son of God.' "

And one of the thieves also which were crucified with him railed on him and cast the same in his teeth, saying, "If thou be Christ, save thyself and us." But the other answering rebuked him, saying, "Dost not thou fear God, seeing thou art in the same condemnation? And we indeed justly; for we receive the due reward of our deeds: but this man hath done nothing amiss." And he said unto Jesus, "Lord, remember me when thou comest into thy kingdom." And Jesus said unto him, "Verily I say unto thee, today shalt thou be with me in paradise."

Now there stood by the cross of Jesus his mother, and his mother's sister, Mary the *wife* of Cleophas, and Mary Magdalene. When Jesus therefore saw his mother, and the disciple standing by, whom he loved, he saith unto his mother, "Woman, behold thy son!" Then saith he to the disciple, "Behold thy mother!" And from that hour that disciple took her unto his own *home.*

And when the sixth hour was come, there was darkness over the whole land until the ninth hour, and the sun was darkened. And about the ninth hour Jesus cried with a loud voice, saying, "Eli, Eli, lama sabachthani?" which is, being interpreted, "My God, my God, why hast thou forsaken me?" Some of them that stood there, when they heard that, said, "Behold he calleth for Elias." After this, Jesus knowing that all things were now accomplished, that the scripture might be fulfilled, saith, "I thirst." Now there was set a vessel full of vinegar: and straightway, one of them ran and took a spunge, and filled it with vinegar, and put it upon a hyssop reed, and put it to his mouth to drink. The rest said, "Let be, let us see whether Elias will come to save him." [take him down—Mark] When Jesus therefore had received the vinegar, he said, "It is finished." And when Jesus had cried again with a loud voice, he said, "Father, into thy hands I commend my spirit": and having said thus, he bowed his head and gave up the ghost.

And behold, the veil of the temple was rent in twain from the top to the bottom; and the earth did quake, and the rocks rent; and the graves were opened; and many bodies of the saints which slept arose, and came out of the graves after his resurrection, and went into the holy city, and appeared unto many. Now when the centurion, and they that were with him, watching Jesus, saw that he so cried out, and gave up the ghost, and saw the earthquake, and those things that were done, they feared greatly and glorified God, saying, "Certainly this was a righteous man, truly this was the Son of God."

The Jews therefore, because it was the preparation, that the bodies should not remain upon the cross on the sabbath day, (for that sabbath day was an high day,) besought Pilate that their legs might be broken, and *that* they might be taken away. Then came the soldiers, and brake the legs of the first, and of the other which was crucified with him. But when they came to Jesus, and saw that he was dead already, they brake not his legs: but one of the soldiers with a spear pierced his side, and forthwith came there out blood and water. And he that saw *it* bare record, and his record is true: and he knoweth that he saith true, that ye might believe. For these things were done, that the scripture should be fulfilled, "A bone of him shall not be broken." And again another scripture saith, "They shall look on him whom they pierced."

And all the people that came together to that sight, beholding the things which were done, smote their breasts, and returned. And all his acquaintance and also many women were there looking on afar off; among whom was Mary Magdalene, and Mary the mother of James the less and of Joses, and the mother of Zebedee's children, and Salome; (who also, when he was in

Galilee, followed him, and ministered unto him;) and many other women which came up with him unto Jerusalem.

And now when the even was come, because it was the preparation, that is, the day before the sabbath, there came a rich man of Arimathaea, a city of the Jews, named Joseph, an honourable counsellor, a good man, and a just: (The same had not consented to the counsel and deed of them;) who also waited for the kingdom of God, who also himself was Jesus' disciple, but secretly for fear of the Jews. This man went boldly unto Pilate and begged that he might take away the body of Jesus. And Pilate marvelled if he were already dead: and calling *unto him* the centurion, he asked him whether he had been any while dead. And when he knew *it* of the centurion, he gave the body to Joseph. And there came also Nicodemus, which at the first came to Jesus by night, and brought a mixture of myrrh and aloes, about an hundred pound *weight*. Then took they down the body of Jesus, and wound it in linen clothes with the spices, as the manner of the Jews is to bury. (Now in the place where he was crucified there was a garden; and in the garden a new sepulchre.) And laid it in his own new tomb wherein never man before was laid, which he had hewn out in the rock: and he rolled a great stone to the door of the sepulchre, and departed. There laid they Jesus therefore because of the Jew's preparation *day*; for the sepulchre was nigh at hand. And the women also, which came with him from Galilee, followed after, and beheld the sepulchre, and how his body was laid. And there was Mary Magdalene, and the other Mary, the *mother* of Joses, sitting over against the sepulchre. And they returned, and prepared spices and ointments; and rested the sabbath day according to the commandment.

Now the next day, that followed the day of the preparation, the chief priests and Pharisees came together unto Pilate, saying, "Sir, we remember that that deceiver said, while he was yet alive, 'After three days I will rise again.' Command therefore that the sepulchre be made sure until the third day, lest his disciples come by night, and steal him away, and say unto the people, 'He is risen from the dead': so the last error shall be worse than the first." Pilate said unto them, "Ye have a watch: go your way, make *it* as sure as ye can." So they went, and made the sepulchre sure, sealing the stone, and setting a watch.

THE RESURRECTION

And when the sabbath was past, Mary Magdalene, out of whom he had cast seven devils, and Mary the *mother* of James, and Salome had bought sweet spices, that they might come and anoint him. The first day of the week, as it began to dawn, when it was yet dark, Mary Magdalene and the other Mary came unto the sepulchre at the rising of the sun, bringing the spices which they and certain *others* with them had prepared. And they said among themselves, "Who shall roll us away the stone from the door of the sepulchre?"

(And, behold, there was a great earthquake: for the angel of the Lord descended from heaven, and came and rolled back the stone from the door, and sat upon it. His countenance was like lightning, and his raiment white as snow: and for fear of him the keepers did shake, and became as dead men.)

And when they looked, they saw that the stone was rolled [taken—John] away from the sepulchre: for it was very great. And they entered in and found not the body of the Lord Jesus. And it came to pass, as they were much perplexed thereabout, behold, two men stood by them in shining garments: they saw one young man sitting on the right side, clothed in a long white garment, and as they were afraid, they bowed down their faces to the earth. And the angel answered and said unto the women, "Fear not ye. I know that ye seek Jesus of Nazareth, which was crucified. Why seek ye the living among the dead? He is not here: he is risen as he said. Come, behold the place where they laid him [where the Lord lay—Matthew]. Remember how he spake unto you when he was yet in Galilee, saying, 'The Son of man must be delivered into the hands of sinful men, and be crucified, and the third day rise again' "* (and they remembered his words). "And go quickly, and tell his disciples and Peter that he is risen from the dead; and, behold, he goeth before you into Galilee; there shall ye see him as he said unto you:† lo, I have told you."

And they departed quickly and fled from the sepulchre with fear and great joy, for they trembled and were amazed: neither said they anything to any *man*; for they were afraid.

(Now when they were going, behold, some of the watch came into the city, and shewed unto the chief priests all the things that were done. And when they were assembled with the elders, and had taken counsel, they gave large money unto the soldiers, saying, "Say ye, 'His disciples came by night, and stole him *away* while we slept.' And if this come to the governor's ears, we will persuade him, and secure you." So they took the money, and did as they were taught: and this saying is commonly reported among the Jews until this day.)

And they did run to bring his disciples word, and told all these things unto the eleven and all the rest. (It was Mary Magdalene, and Joanna, and Mary *the mother* of James, and other *women that were* with them, which told these things unto the apostles. And their words seemed to them as idle tales, and they believed not.) And as they went to tell his disciples, behold, Jesus met them, saying, "All hail." And they came and held him by the feet, and worshipped him. Then said Jesus unto them, "Be not afraid: go tell my brethren that they go into Galilee, and there shall they see me."

Meanwhile,‡ Mary runneth, and cometh to Simon Peter, and

---

*See p. 93.
†See p. 151.
‡I have added this word to clarify what seems to be the order of events. A group of women, led by Mary Magdalene and Mary the mother of James, went first to the sepulchre and received the message of the resurrection. They also received instruction to tell the disciples (with Peter indicated separately—Mark). Mary Magdalene went directly to tell Peter and John, while the others went to

to the other disciple, whom Jesus loved, and saith unto them, "They have taken away the Lord out of the sepulchre, and we know not where they have laid him." Then Peter arose and went forth and that other disciple, and came to the sepulchre. So they ran both together: and the other disciple did outrun Peter, and came first to the sepulchre. And he, stooping down, *and looking in*, saw the linen clothes lying; yet went he not in. Then cometh Simon Peter following him, and stooping down, went into the sepulchre and saw the linen clothes laid by themselves. And the napkin, that was about his head, not lying with the linen clothes, but wrapped together in a place by itself. Then went in also that other disciple, which came first to the sepulchre, and he saw, and believed. For as yet they knew not the scripture, that he must rise again from the dead. Then the disciples went away again unto their own home. And Peter departed wondering in himself at that which was come to pass.

But Mary stood without at the sepulchre weeping: and as she wept, she stooped down, *and looked* into the sepulchre, and seeth two angels in white sitting, the one at the head, and the other at the feet, where the body of Jesus had lain. And they say unto her, "Woman, why weepest thou?" She saith unto them, "Because they have taken away my Lord, and I know not where they have laid him." And when she had thus said, she turned herself back, and saw Jesus standing, and knew not that it was Jesus. Jesus saith unto her, "Woman, why weepest thou? whom seekest thou?" She, supposing him to be the gardener, saith unto him, "Sir, if thou have borne him hence, tell me where thou hast laid him, and I will take him away." Jesus saith unto her, "Mary." She turned herself, and saith unto him. "Rabboni"; which is to say, "Master." Jesus saith unto her,

the place where the other disciples were gathered. Thus, the separate meetings of Jesus with Mary Magdalene and with the other women is explained. From Mark we learn that Mary's encounter with Jesus occurs before that of the other women, but I have not tried to alter the sequence of the passages to show that, as it would have meant adding more transitional wording.

"Touch me not*: for I am not yet ascended to my Father: but go to my brethren, and say unto them, I ascend unto my Father, and your Father; and *to* my God, and your God." Mary Magdalene came and told the disciples, as they mourned and wept, that she had seen the Lord, and *that* he had spoken these things unto her.† And they, when they had heard that he was alive, and had been seen of her, believed not.

JOURNEY TO EMMAUS

And, behold, two of them went that same day to a village called Emmaus, which was from Jerusalem *about* threescore furlongs. And they talked together of all these things which had happened. And it came to pass, that, while they communed *together* and reasoned, Jesus himself drew near, and went with them. But their eyes were holden that they should not know him. And he said unto them, "What manner of communications *are* these that ye have one to another, as ye walk, and are sad?" And the one of them, whose name was Cleopas, answering said unto him, "Art thou only a stranger in Jerusalem, and hast not known the things which are come to pass there in these days?" And he said them, "What things?" And they said unto him, "Concerning Jesus of Nazareth, which was a prophet mighty in deed and word before God and all the people: and how the chief priests and our rulers delivered him to be condemned to death, and have crucified him. But we trusted that it had been he which should have redeemed Israel: and beside all this, to day is the third day since these things were done. Yea, and certain women also of our company made us astonished, which were

---

*It is significant that of all his disciples and followers, only Mary is not allowed to touch Jesus. He even urges the rest to make physical contact.

†There is no reason to suppose that this passage in John refers to more than Peter and John.

early at the sepulchre; and when they found not his body, they came, saying, that they had also seen a vision of angels, which said that he was alive. And certain of them which were with us went to the sepulchre, and found *it* even so as the women had said: but him they saw not." Then he said unto them, "O fools, and slow of heart to believe all that the prophets have spoken: ought not Christ to have suffered these things, and to enter into his glory?" And beginning at Moses and all the prophets, he expounded unto them in all the scriptures the things concerning himself. And they drew nigh unto the village whither they went: and he made as though he would have gone further. But they constrained him, saying, "Abide with us: for it is toward evening, and the day is far spent." And he went in to tarry with them. And it came to pass, as he sat at meat with them, he took bread, and blessed *it*, and brake, and gave to them. And their eyes were opened, and they knew him; and he vanished out of their sight. And they said one to another, "Did not our heart burn within us, while he talked with us by the way, and while he opened to us the scriptures?" And they rose up the same hour, and returned to Jerusalem, and found the eleven gathered together, and them that were with them, saying, "The Lord is risen indeed, and hath appeared to Simon." And they told what things *were done* in the way, and how he was known of them in breaking of bread; neither believed they them.

APPEARANCE TO THE DISCIPLES

Then the same day at evening, being the first day of the week, as they sat at meat, when the doors were shut where the disciples were assembled for fear of the Jews, came Jesus and stood in the midst, and saith unto them, "Peace be unto you," and upbraided them with their unbelief and hardness of heart, because they believed not them which had seen him after he was risen. But they were terrified and affrighted, and supposed that they had seen a spirit. And he said unto them, "Why are ye troubled? and why do thoughts arise in your hearts? Behold my hands and my feet, that it is I myself: handle me, and see; for a spirit hath not flesh and bones, as ye see me have." And when he had thus spoken, he shewed them his hands and his feet and his side. Then were the disciples glad, when they saw the Lord. And while they yet believed not for joy, and wondered, he said unto them, "Have ye here any meat?" And they gave him a piece of a broiled fish, and of an honeycomb. And he took *it*, and did eat before them. And he said unto them, "These *are* the words which I spake unto you, while I was yet with you, that all things must be fulfilled, which were written in the law of Moses, and *in* the prophets, and *in* the psalms, concerning me." Then opened he their understanding, that they might understand the scriptures, and said unto them, "Thus it is written, and thus it behoved Christ to suffer, and to rise from the dead the third day; and that repentance and remission of sins should be preached in his name among all nations, beginning at Jerusalem. And ye are witnesses of these things. And, behold, I send the promise of my Father upon you: but tarry ye in the city of Jerusalem until ye be endued with power from on high." Then said Jesus to them again, "Peace be unto you: as my Father hath sent me, even so send I you." And when he had said this, he breathed on *them*, and saith unto them, "Receive ye the Holy Ghost: Whose soever sins ye remit, they are remitted unto them; *and* whose soever *sins* ye retain, they are retained."

DOUBTING THOMAS

But Thomas, one of the twelve, called Didymus, was not with them when Jesus came. The other disciples therefore said unto him, "We have seen the Lord." But he said unto them, "Except I shall see in his hands the print of the nails, and put my finger into the print of the nails, and thrust my hand into his side, I will not believe." And after eight days again his disciples were within, and Thomas with them: *then* came Jesus, the doors being shut, and stood in the midst, and said, "Peace *be* unto you." Then saith he to Thomas, "Reach hither thy finger, and behold my hands; and reach hither thy hand, and thrust *it* into my side: and be not faithless, but believing." And Thomas answered and said unto him, "My Lord and my God." Jesus saith unto him, "Thomas, because thou hast seen me, thou hast believed: blessed are they that have not seen, and *yet* have believed." Then said Jesus unto them, "Be not afraid: go tell my brethren that they go into Galilee, and there shall they see me." And he led them out as far as to Bethany, and he lifted up his hands, and blessed them.

And many other signs truly did Jesus in the presence of his disciples, which are not written in this book; but these are written, that ye might believe that Jesus is the Christ, the Son of God; and that believing ye might have life through his name.

APPEARANCE IN GALILEE

After these things Jesus shewed himself again to the disciples at the sea of Tiberias; and on this wise shewed he *himself.* There were together Simon Peter, and Thomas called Didymus, and Nathanael of Cana in Galilee, and the *sons* of Zebedee, and two other of his disciples. Simon Peter saith unto them, "I go a fishing." They say unto him, "We also go with thee." They went forth, and entered into a ship immediately: and that night they caught nothing. But when the morning was now come, Jesus stood on the shore: but the disciples knew not that it was Jesus. Then Jesus saith unto them, "Children, have ye any meat?" They answered him, "No." And he said unto them, "Cast the net on the right side of the ship, and ye shall find." They cast therefore, and now they were not able to draw it for the multitude of fishes. Therefore that disciple whom Jesus loved saith unto

Peter, "It is the Lord." Now when Simon Peter heard that it was the Lord, he girt *his* fisher's coat *unto him,* (for he was naked,) and did cast himself into the sea. And the disciples came in a little ship; (for they were not far from land, but as it were two hundred cubits,) dragging the net with fishes. As soon then as they were come to land, they saw a fire of coals there, and fish laid thereon, and bread. Jesus saith unto them, "Bring of the fish which ye have now caught." Simon Peter went up, and drew the net to land full of great fishes, an hundred and fifty and three: and for all there were so many, yet was not the net broken. Jesus saith unto them, "Come *and* dine." And none of the disciples durst ask him, "Who art thou?" knowing that it was the Lord. Jesus then cometh, and taketh bread, and giveth them, and fish likewise. This is now the third time that Jesus shewed himself to his disciples, after that he was risen from the dead.

So when they had dined, Jesus saith to Simon Peter, "Simon, *son* of Jonas, lovest thou me more than these?" He saith unto him, "Yea, Lord; thou knowest that I love thee." He saith unto him, "Feed my lambs." He saith to him again the second time, "Simon, *son* of Jonas, lovest thou me?" He saith unto him, "Yea, Lord; thou knowest that I love thee." He saith unto him, "Feed my sheep." He saith unto him the third time, "Simon, *son* of Jonas, lovest thou me?" Peter was grieved because he said unto him the third time, "Lovest thou me?" And he said unto him, "Lord, thou knowest all things; thou knowest that I love thee." Jesus saith unto him, "Feed my sheep. Verily, verily, I say unto thee, When thou wast young, thou girdest thyself, and walkedst whither thou wouldest: but when thou shalt be old, thou shalt stretch forth thy hands, and another shall gird thee, and carry *thee* whither thou wouldest not." This spake he, signifying by what death he should glorify God. And when he had spoken this, he saith unto him, "Follow me." Then Peter, turning about, seeth the disciple whom Jesus loved following; which also leaned on his breast at supper, and said, "Lord, which is he that betrayeth thee?" Peter seeing him saith to Jesus, "Lord, and what *shall* this man *do?*" Jesus saith unto him, "If I will that he tarry till I come, what *is that* to thee? follow thou me." Then went this saying abroad among the brethren, that that disciple should not die: yet Jesus said not unto him, "He shall not die"; but, "If I will that he tarry till I come, what *is that* to thee?" This is the disciple which testifieth of these things, and wrote these things: and we know that his testimony is true. And there are also many other things which Jesus did, the which, if they should be written every one, I suppose that even the world itself could not contain the books that should be written. Amen.

And he said unto them, "Go ye into all the world, and preach the gospel to every creature. He that believeth and is baptized shall be saved; but he that believeth not shall be damned. And these signs shall follow them that believe; In my name shall they cast out devils; they shall speak with new tongues; they shall take up serpents; and if they drink any deadly thing, it shall not hurt them; they shall lay hands on the sick, and they shall recover."

THE ASCENSION

Then the eleven disciples went away into Galilee, into a mountain where Jesus had appointed them. And when they saw him, they worshipped him: but some doubted. And Jesus came and spake unto them, saying, "All power is given unto me in heaven and in earth. Go ye therefore, and teach all nations, baptizing them in the name of the Father, and of the Son, and of the Holy Ghost: teaching them to observe all things whatsoever I have commanded you: and, lo, I am with you always, *even* unto the end of the world. Amen." And it came to pass, while he blessed them, he was parted from them, and carried up into heaven, and sat on the right hand of God. And they worshipped him, and returned to Jerusalem with great joy: and were continually in the temple, praising and blessing God. And they went forth, and preached every where, the Lord working with *them*, and confirming the word with signs following. Amen.